Matt,

Love Dad & Mom

Christmas 2004

In New Mexico

MORE ADVANCE PRAISE FOR REPOSITIONING ASIA: FROM BUBBLE TO SUSTAINABLE ECONOMY

Repositioning Asia appropriately positions itself with its back to the recent crisis and looking ahead to recovery and growth. The authors provide an interesting interpretation of the Asian crisis, but the strength of this book is its forward-looking analysis. Taking a cue from the Chinese word for crisis which means both danger and opportunity, the authors argue that the future is bright for those who are willing to learn and adapt. The chapters on revitalization strategy should be particularly useful for managers and policy makers in Asia and abroad.

Dilip Ratha
Senior Economist, World Bank

No job in the world is more difficult than turning the Asian economies around. Phil Kotler and Hermawan Kartajaya have teamed up for the first time to tackle this tough task. They have done a fine job in isolating the nature of the problem and outlining the solutions.

Al Ries
Chairman, Ries & Ries
Co-author, **Positioning: The Battle For Your Mind**

The book provides profound insights into the root causes of Asia's crisis and the economic sustainability of crisis-hit countries. A crisis is a time to see opportunities in every challenge. Companies will grow and sustain in the long run, if they possess vision, entrepreneurship and ability to learn, unlearn as well as anticipate the pace of change.

Dr Mochtar Riady
Chairman, Lippo Group

To concentrate on a specific field of business and to keep on trying in building competency, as well as to continuously anticipating changes in the business landscape are not easy tasks. However, this has to be achieved so that a company can constantly grow and develop. This is the important message extracted from the book.

Stan Shih
Chairman, Acer Group

Repositioning Asia

Repositioning Asia

From Bubble to Sustainable Economy

PHILIP KOTLER

J.L. Kellogg Graduate School of Management
Northwestern University

HERMAWAN KARTAJAYA

MarkPlus Strategy Consulting

John Wiley & Sons (Asia) Pte Ltd
Singapore • New York • Chichester • Weinheim • Brisbane • Toronto

Copyright © 2000 by John Wiley & Sons (Asia) Pte Ltd
Published in 2000 by John Wiley & Sons (Asia) Pte Ltd
2 Clementi Loop, #02-01, Singapore 129809

This publication is designed to provide accurate and authoritative information in regard to the
subject matter covered. It is sold with the understanding that the publisher is not engaged in rendering
professional services. If professional advice or other expert assistance is required, the services of a
competent professional person should be sought.

Other Wiley Editorial Offices

John Wiley & Sons, Inc., 605 Third Avenue, New York, NY 10158-0012, USA
John Wiley & Sons Ltd, Baffins Lane, Chichester, West Sussex PO19 1UD, England
John Wiley & Sons (Canada) Ltd, 22 Worcester Road, Rexdale, Ontario M9W 1L1, Canada
John Wiley & Sons Australia Ltd, 33 Park Road (PO Box 1226), Milton, Queensland 4064,
Australia
Wiley-VCH, Pappelallee 3, 69469 Weinheim, Germany

Library of Congress Cataloging-in-Publication Data

Kotler, Philip.
    Repositioning Asia: from bubble to sustainable economy / Philip Kotler, Hermawan Kartajaya.
        p. cm.
    Includes index.
    ISBN 0-471-84665-1 (cloth: alk. paper)
    1. Asia–Economic conditions–1945.   2. Asia–Economic policy–Decision making.
    3.   Industrial management–Asia. I. Kartajaya, Hermawan, 1947–

HC412.K66 2000
338.95–dc21

                                                                00-028974

Typeset in 11/14 points, Palatino by Linographic Services Pte Ltd
Printed in Singapore by Craft Print International Ltd
10 9 8 7 6 5 4 3 2 1

CONTENTS

FOREWORD

It's hard to imagine that Asia has recently undergone change of a great magnitude. The Asian economic crisis, which began with the devaluation of the Thai baht in early July 1997, inauspiciously a day after the return of Hong Kong to China, has taken its toll on small and large businesses alike, transcending local and multinational corporate status, regardless of nationality and industry. Although the financial storm has abated somewhat and signs of recovery are evident, individuals, firms, and governments will benefit from an understanding of how such a crisis started and of the strategies that they can undertake to ensure that they can see their way through similar crises and emerge relatively stronger in the new millennium.

Repositioning Asia: From Bubble to Sustainable Economy encapsulates both the problems and lessons of the Asian crisis. It also provides a learning perspective for both governments and companies operating in Asia. Recovery strategies are presented to provide guidelines on how they can climb out of the mire and prepare for the challenges of the "new economy," while preventive strategies are suggested to minimize the reoccurrence of similar crises.

Andersen Consulting is very proud to sponsor *Repositioning Asia*, which is co-authored by two world-renowned experts and strategists: Professor Philip Kotler and

Hermawan Kartajaya. This book is in line with our commitment to take a major part in the recovery process in Asia and is consistent with our mission, which is *to help our clients create their future*.

Enjoy the book!

Larry Gan
Asia Managing Partner, Andersen Consulting

When the financial crisis hit Asia in 1997, most people expected the region to be reduced to ruins. What had been the fastest-growing economy in the world was suddenly seen as the worst place for investment. Many commentators were quick to point the finger of blame for the crisis. Macroeconomists blamed Asia's failure on its macroeconomic policies. Banking and financial analysts pointed to Asia's weak financial systems. The cause of the Asian crisis may have been in dispute, but its result was not: the Asian miracle appeared to be over.

The Chinese character for "crisis" (see below) is pronounced *wei-ji* and means both "danger" and "opportunity."

To understand the Asian crisis, which forms Part I of this book, one must first understand the Asian ways of economic development. The letters that make up the word "Asian" could be said to stand for:

Authoritarian government
State-led development
Institutionalization
Asian values
Network

Most of the nations in Asia have based their growth on these five elements. *Authoritarian government* isn't necessarily bad. For example, Singapore's government is often criticized as being authoritarian, but it is also lean, clean, and efficient. One reason for this is that government officials are well paid. The Prime Minister of Singapore is the highest-paid head of government in the world. Soeharto, who ruled Indonesia with an iron-fist for 32 years, and Malaysia's Prime Minister Mahathir Mohammad are other authoritarian figures. The People's Republic of China with its single party (the Communist Party) is another example of an authoritarian government.

State-led development is a characteristic of most Asian countries. Japan's Ministry of International Trade and Industry (MITI), for example, is very powerful in selecting industries for development. South Korea, which has a "hate–love" relationship with Japan, is a strong follower of the Japanese development model. For example, many of its *chaebols* are based on the *keiretsu* model in Japan. The Singapore government, which manages a large public sector, also takes an active role in the city-state's economic development. Most Asian governments are directly involved in their country's industries and businesses.

An authoritarian government pushing state-led development is typical of Asia's *institutions*. Asians have their own models of governance, financial, and legal institutions, and transparency is not always a high priority. Often, informal institutions are much more powerful than the formal ones. Although Asian institutions vary from country to country, there is a high degree of similarity among them.

Asian values, such as managing good relationships (*guanxi*), maintaining family cohesion, and upholding harmony, were initially praised as contributing to Asia's rapid development during the boom period. *Networks*, especially the overseas Chinese network, also played an important role in Asia's economic development. The overseas Chinese have been a major engine of growth in almost all Southeast Asian countries, just as the Japanese network (*keiretsu*) has created much growth in Asia. But the Japanese network is a corporate network, while the overseas Chinese network is a community network. In South Asia, we also see an Indian-ethnic network driving economic development.

These five elements, then, can be said to account for Asia's growth until the crisis struck. Now let's look at the letters that comprise the word "crisis."

Currency
Response
Information
State-driven economy
Investment
Sustainable

The Asian crisis started with a *currency* crisis. Asia, which had been a favored region for investors, became a target for currency speculators. The Asian currencies became overvalued and volatile, and the signs began to indicate a "bubble economy."

The more of a "bubble" an economy is, the more difficult it is for a government to *respond* in the right way. When governments undertook efforts to defend their exchange rates, the business community and the general public became alarmed. Panic set in and negative *information* about the situation spread quickly.

The opportunity part came when Asian governments took steps to calm the situation and undertake recovery and reform efforts. Most Asian economies became *state-driven*. The fragile banking industry was capitalized; some banks were even taken over by the government. The same thing happened to private companies that could not pay their debts.

Afterwards, new *investments*, especially foreign invest-ments, were invited to "save" many domestic businesses in various industries. It was hoped that foreign investors would restructure these troubled companies in an effort to create *sustainable* enterprises.

This explains the title of this book, *Repositioning Asia: From Bubble to Sustainable Economy*. Without the Asian crisis, Asia might still be a "bubble" region without any incentive to carry out creative destruction and reform. The crisis has given Asia the opportunity to relaunch itself as a "sustainable" economy. The repositioning efforts need to be done at both the country level and the company level. In the post-crisis era, we strongly believe that Asia will be much stronger than before.

The book is divided into three parts. Part I presents important background information on the Asian crisis. We describe how the crisis unfolded and analyze its root causes, reviewing explanations from various experts. Chapter 1 presents the complexity of the issue and the difficulty of pinpointing a single, comprehensive explanation of the subject.

Part II contains three chapters that propose how Asian nations should proceed to renew and reposition themselves. In Chapter 2, we explain that Asian economies can renew themselves into sustainable economies. In Chapter 3, we discuss how Asia can reposition itself in the changing and dynamic "globalized" world. In Chapter 4, we will indicate how Asia can reorganize itself in order to become a sustainable region.

Part III contains three chapters that explain how companies operating in Asia (both Asian and multinational companies) can revitalize themselves and even take advantage of the opportunities provided by the crisis. Chapter 5 groups Asian companies into four categories: bubble companies, aggressive companies, conservative companies, and sustainable companies. It is our contention that bubble, aggressive, and conservative companies must move toward becoming sustainable companies, which are companies that continually adapt to the ever-changing market. While Chapter 5 describes what Asian companies should do, Chapter 6 explains how they can revitalize themselves using the sustainable marketing enterprise model, which is a comprehensive strategic business framework that was created by Hermawan Kartajaya to help revitalize many companies in Indonesia and several others in Asia. Finally, Chapter 7 discusses issues (challenges and opportunities) that are faced by multinational companies in Asia. It also presents a generic formula that can be used by the MNCs to succeed in the region.

Philip Kotler
Hermawan Kartajaya
June 2000

ACKNOWLEDGMENTS

Many people have assisted with the research for this book, but two people, Michael Hermawan and Taufik, deserve special mention for their dedication to the project. Michael Hermawan took leave from his job at Andersen Consulting to work on the project for eight months. And in the last three months of researching, writing, and revising the book, Taufik left his position as managing publication executive at MarkPlus to join the team, contributing his "encyclopedic mind" and extensive knowledge of macroeconomics.

We would also like to thank Andersen Consulting for their support in permitting Michael Hermawan to join this project and for assisting us with the research for and promotion of the book. We want especially to thank Glenn H. Bryce, Dermot McMeekin, Heru Prasetyo, and other partners in the Asia-Pacific offices who have been so supportive of this project. We would also like to thank Yeo Guan-Kai and Nia Sarinastiti, who facilitated and organized the promotion activities for the book. And last but not least, we wish to thank those analysts and consultants who assisted us in locating important data and articles. In particular, we wish to thank Martin Wong Tai-Foo of the Kuala Lumpur office.

We benefited greatly from a number of friends and colleagues who sent us their latest studies and articles. Michael Hamlin of TeamAsia (author of *The New Asian Corporation*) supplied us with many excellent case studies for the book:

1. The Myth & Reality of Malaysia's Capital Controls (p. 31)
2. Japan: No Longer Doomed (p. 69)
3. We Believe in Him (p. 83)
4. Growing the New Asian Economy (p. 100)
5. Hard Decisions in the New Asian Economy (p. 126)
6. PLDT: Revitalizing a state-owned Telecom company (p. 147)

Linda Lim, director of the Southeast Asia Business Program at the University of Michigan, kindly made available to us her insightful articles and thoughts on the Asian crisis. Dr. Gerald Delilkhan, general manager of KS Graduate Business School, St. Gallen, contributed his latest study on Hong Kong. Cheong Kun Pui, managing director of MarkPlus International Ltd. (Singapore), sent us relevant articles from time to time. We also value the articles sent by our friends and colleagues at the Asia Pacific Marketing Federation and the World Marketing Association.

We received immense help from several others on the staff at MarkPlus. We wish to thank Agus Santoso, Yuswohady (Siwo), Jacky Mussry, Anneke Rina, and Sandra Cahyadi. We are particularly thankful to Agus and Siwo, who spent tireless hours designing and configuring the "cosmetic" layout of the manuscript.

To our spouses, Nancy Kotler and Suliawati Santoso, thank you for supporting us as we struggled through the long months of writing. We are eternally grateful to you.

We would also like to acknowledge our debt to Nick Wallwork and Janis Soo of John Wiley & Sons (Asia) Pte Ltd, who supported us from the beginning. Their constructive feedback made this book much better than the original manuscript. We would also like to thank Robyn Flemming for her superb copy-editing, as well as Adeline Lim, Audrey Wee, and Li Li Teo of the marketing department for their fine job in promoting this book.

PART
I

Background

CHAPTER 1

UNDERSTANDING THE ASIAN CRISIS

For many in Hong Kong, the early hours of July 1, 1997 were a time for revelry. A lavish celebration was held to commemorate the handover of the city-state from Great Britain to the People's Republic of China. Two separate ceremonies were held within hours of each other at the futuristic Convention and Exhibition Centre. The festivities ranged from an extravagant fireworks display to a US$13 million pyrotechnic and laser display over Victoria Harbour. In front of dignitaries from all around the world, Tung Chee-hwa, the new leader of the Hong Kong Special Administrative Region (SAR), proudly heralded the "new era and new identity" for Hong Kong.[1] Witnesses to this extravagant celebration could be forgiven for not detecting that the "worst crisis since the Second World War"[2] was imminent.

How the Crisis Unfolded

Several months prior to the Hong Kong celebrations, several Asian countries, particularly Thailand, had begun to sense but deliberately ignored early warning signs of the crisis. In Thailand, the current account deficit hit a high of 8% of GDP and many firms faced bankruptcy as interest rates continued to climb. In June 1997, the Thai stock market plunged to its lowest level in eight years. Sixteen finance firms were suspended in order to arrange mergers with healthier entities.[3] In the midst of this, the Thai government vowed to prop up the baht lest Thais "all become poor."[4]

On July 2, the day after the celebrations of the Hong Kong handover, the baht plunged as the Thai government announced a managed float on the currency, effectively admitting defeat in the wake of an attack by speculators that had lasted for several months. This was the first official day of the Asian crisis. It was unforeseen and unexpected.

The subsequent events resembled the eruption of Krakatoa, a volcano located between the islands of Java and Sumatra in Indonesia. When Krakatoa last erupted, on August 27, 1883, the force of the explosion destroyed most of the volcano itself and created a 100-foot high tidal wave. Cities in the vicinity of the explosion were plunged into darkness, and ash and debris covered an area of around 300,000 square miles. The eruption was heard as far away as the Philippines, Alice Springs in Australia, Rodriguez Island, and Madagascar, and it was reported that ash even reached the west coast of the United States.

Similarly, the Asian crisis occurred in three sequential phases: the ASEAN (Association of South East Asian Nations) meltdown, the Asian "explosion," and the global "aftershock."[5] The crisis first "erupted" in Thailand when the government devalued the baht in mid-July 1997. The ill-effects of this "eruption" then spread to Thailand's neighboring ASEAN countries. It was at this stage that many people experienced the initial shocks. Yet, others remained in denial. The "fallout" continued, however, as the ASEAN meltdown spread to other East Asian countries, including South Korea, Hong Kong, and even Vietnam. By the beginning of 1998, the Asian markets experienced a brief period of rebound, but then the "aftershock" occurred.

During the aftershock phase, the Asian crisis was not limited to only countries in Asia only, but also other countries around the world, creating fears of a global meltdown. In

Indonesia, the economic problems exacerbated other problems, producing civil and political unrest. This is the stage during which Asians began to accept that they were experiencing a debilitating crisis. In fact, it was during this stage that talk of the need for serious restructuring efforts began to emerge. A more detailed account of the major events during the Asian crisis is set out in Table 1.1.

Table 1.1: Chronology of the Asian Crisis

The ASEAN Meltdown

• May–June 1997	Thai baht under severe speculative attacks; Bank of Thailand intervened aggressively
• July 2, 1997	Thai baht devalued to 28.80 per US$ as Bank of Thailand announced managed float of the baht (trigger of the Asian crisis)
• July 11, 1997	Philippines allowed peso to float; Indonesia widened rupiah's trading band from 8% to 12%
• July 17, 1997	Singapore dollar depreciated to 1.46 per US$, its lowest level since February 1995
• July 24, 1997	Malaysia's ringgit hit a 38-month low of 2.65 per US$; PM Mahathir verbally attacked "rogue speculators"
• August 3, 1997	Malaysia cut foreign access to the ringgit through swap deals
• August 13, 1997	Indonesia abolished trading bands; rupiah fell to 2,740 per US$

The Asian Explosion

• July 1997	The Hong Kong Monetary Authority (HKMA) spent US$1 billion to fight off speculators' attacks on the HK dollar
• August 15, 1997	HKMA raised interest rates by 150 basis points to 8%; Hang Seng Index fell by 2.4% in response
• September 1997	ASEAN currencies slumped further
• October 17, 1997	ASEAN contagion spread to Taiwan dollar, which dropped by 5% to 29.89 per US$
• October 20–24, 1997	Hang Seng Index shed more than 23% over the period
• October 27, 1997	Wall Street fell by 554 points
• October 31, 1997	Indonesia signed a US$23 billion rescue plan with the IMF; central bank closed 16 banks
• November 6, 1997	Korean won slid despite government intervention; financial system's health was questioned
• November 9, 1997	Thailand's political paralysis ends with appointment of Chuan Leek Pai as prime minister
• November 17–21, 1997	Korean government stopped defending the won and signed a US$57 billion rescue package with the IMF
• November 24, 1997	Yamaichi Securities declared bankruptcy
• December 18, 1997	Kim Dae Jung won presidency in Korea

Table 1.1 (cont'd)

The Global Aftershock

• January 5, 1998	Indonesia's President Soeharto signed a second agreement with the IMF
• January 12, 1998	Hong Kong's Peregrine Investments failed
• January 16–19, 1998	Most Asian stock markets and currencies showed strong rebound during this period
• January 22, 1998	Indonesia's rupiah plunged to 15,000 per US$
• February 10, 1998	President Soeharto told of his plan for a currency board system (CBS), which would peg the rupiah to US$; IMF shunned the idea
• March 10, 1998	Students' protests began in Indonesia over hunger
• March 20, 1998	Soeharto shelved the CBS proposal and initiated new talks with IMF
• May 12–14, 1998	Riots erupted in Jakarta after security forces killed four students
• May 19, 1998	Stock markets in Russia, Brazil, Mexico, and Argentina plunged
• May 21, 1998	Soeharto resigned; Vice-President B.J. Habibie took over
• May 29, 1998	Hong Kong announced a 2% contraction in first quarter
• June 8, 1998	Japan's yen fell to below 140 per US$; worries over Chinese yuan's devaluation emerged
• August–October 1988	Fear of global meltdown emerged as Russia's crisis rippled to Latin America
• October–November 1998	Recovery of investors' confidence

Sources: Asiaweek and Nouriel Roubini's Asian crisis website (http://www.stern.nyu.edu/
~nroubini/asia/AsiaHomepage.html).

What Caused the Asian Crisis?

As the crisis unfolded, many people in Asia saw disturbing parallels between their countries' economies and the fate of the "unsinkable" *Titanic*, subject of a blockbuster movie at the time. Like the *Titanic*, Asia had been considered a miracle by the world. Investors, both foreign and domestic, had flocked into the region with high hopes of exploiting the abundant opportunities to be found there. Phenomenal economic growth performances through the 1980s and 1990s attracted even more money, and overconfidence became pervasive. Companies, enjoying easy access to foreign loans, rushed to invest in the region, often with little or only superficial due diligence. This overconfidence lasted for several years, leading to the phenomenon dubbed the *Asian miracle*.

Like those on the *Titanic*, everyone was still partying when disaster struck. Suddenly, Asians realized what had happened and, panic-stricken, scrambled to save their own lives. For many people, it was already too late. Others got out of the region in time to save themselves or to invest elsewhere. A few smart ones were able to take advantage of the mayhem as those around them were sinking.

The Asian crisis is now generally thought to be over. Some commentators, in fact, date the beginning of recovery back to early 1999. A number of countries that had suffered badly have begun to show signs of returning to their "miraculous" selves. This has encouraged global investors who suffered heavy losses in 1997–98 to begin making major investments in the region again, even though appropriate systems and business practices are not yet fully in place.

Of course, with the end of the crisis, people have begun to look at ways of avoiding a repeat performance. These efforts will only be effective if we can gain a good understanding of what caused the crisis in the first place. The Asian crisis had varying impact on East Asian countries. Some economies experienced only a slight drop in macroeconomic performance, while for others, the crisis changed their whole socioeconomic landscape.

Clearly, the region is heterogeneous in nature — a fact not previously appreciated. Conventional wisdom held that, largely owing to similar macroeconomic growth rates, they were a homogeneous group of nations that adhered to the same model for economic development and were tightly bound by geographical proximity and social harmony. This is the reason why "herding" behavior occurred when the crisis struck. On seeing Thailand's currency collapse, investors immediately pulled out their capital from other Asian countries. The very different effects of the crisis on each country, however, make it difficult to ascribe the crisis to a single root cause. Many books, papers, and commentaries have nevertheless attempted to do so. In general, the failures of both Western systems, such as the open market and democracy, and the Asian development model, are thought to be the main factors. However, Linda Y.C. Lim, Professor of International Business and Director of the Southeast Asian Business Program at the University of Michigan's Business School, explains in her paper, "Whose 'Model' Failed? Implications of the Asian Economic Crisis,"[6] that the real cause of the crisis is far more complex. There was, she says, no simple cause.

For this reason, we will attempt to identify all of the significant contributive factors. We will begin by explaining how the Asian miracle developed in the first place, pinpointing both the positives and negatives of the Asian development process. We will then refer to Professor Lim's paper, which illustrates very clearly the controversy between the Western and Asian models. Finally, because we are both marketing people by profession, we will discuss the crisis from a marketing perspective, using the nation's capability model which received widespread attention following publication of Kotler et al.'s book, *The Marketing of Nations*, in 1997.[7]

The Road to the Asian Miracle

The Emergence of Japanese Leadership

Unlike other regions previously under the yoke of colonial rule, Asia showed swift and dramatic changes, as is evidenced by the numerous new nation-states that sprang up across the region after gaining independence. The fact is, after the fall of colonialism, conditions in Asia were more favorable than elsewhere. Asia possessed an abundance of resources, both human and natural, and, with the exception of Indochina and the Middle East, it was generally more successful in achieving sociopolitical stability than were other colonized regions, particularly Africa.

Thus, economic development in Asia was more rapid and more durable, lasting right up until the crisis. The development process, however, did not come at a uniform pace. Each Asian nation had different degrees of opportunity to initiate its own development process.

Japan was the first Asian nation to undergo a process of development through modernization. This began after the seat of power — which since 1192 had been controlled by the *Shogun*, a succession of military governments — was restored to the imperial court in 1867. The first of the new emperors was Mutsuhito, alias Meiji Tenno (1867–1912).

Japan's efforts to modernize covered four main areas: government, education, the economy, and the armed forces. The results were extraordinary. Japan not only succeeded in reversing the loss of face it had suffered as a result of the Shimoda Agreement, but also managed to bend countries such as Russia and China to its will. Russia was even defeated in its war with Japan in 1905.

However, these developments gave rise to overconfidence. Japan then sought to extend its range of influence, to establish new markets for its products, and to secure new homes for its citizens. The Japanese embarked on a policy of regional imperialism not long after the Tanaka Memorial in 1927, which visualized a prosperous, united Asia. This imperialist policy lasted until the Japanese surrendered at the end of World War II in 1945.

Japan's defeat led to increased efforts to restrict the country's military capability to a self-defensive role. But in other areas, there was little change in policy. Despite the devastation left by the war, Japanese industry rose to prominence again in a very short time. To provide an outlet for its industriousness, the country naturally needed to look for markets once again. Since it was still the target of widespread sanctions following its defeat, it switched tactics from a "security" approach to a "prosperity" approach.

In order to market their new products, the Japanese planned to encourage other Asian countries to transform their agrarian-based economies into industry-based ones. By doing this, they hoped to relocate those industries in which they could not compete, especially as a result of rising labor costs, to neighboring countries. Those countries that succeeded in effecting structural transformation would then do the same to other Asian countries. Of course, countries that were successful would raise their per capita GDP, and thus be ripe for the establishment and development of markets for Japanese products.

The "Flying Geese" Phenomenon

The steps taken by Japan to encourage this structural transformation were further developed by the suggestions put forward by the economist Kaname Akamasu in the 1930s, regarding the international division of labor as a part of the pattern of dynamic economic development that was engulfing Asia. Akamasu used the example of geese flying in formation as a way of conveying his message in simple terms (see Figure 1.1). Geese in temperate countries fly together in a "V" formation headed by one goose, which will lead them to a place where conditions are more favorable. The "flying geese" phenomenon

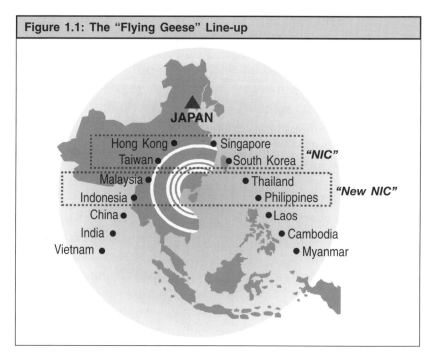

Figure 1.1: The "Flying Geese" Line-up

achieved worldwide publicity in the 1960s after the publication of an article in English on the subject.[8]

In spite of this, the concept only became popular in the 1980s following the rapid Japan-led economic growth throughout Asia. An explanation of this phenomenon, with reference to Akamasu's original concept, was presented by the Japanese economist Saburo Okita at the Pacific Economic Cooperation Conference in 1985.[9]

Flying in a "V" formation, the geese highlight the differences between the economic levels of the various Asian countries. Countries toward the front tend to transfer "older" industries to countries at the back. This process is continuous because of changes in comparative superiority. According to Okita, these dynamic changes throughout the Asian region led to correspondingly dynamic changes in the division of labor, as illustrated by the flying geese. The division of labor in Asia follows a different pattern from the horizontal pattern found in Western Europe, which is marked by trade in manufactured goods between countries that are more or less at the same stage of industrial development and have similar cultural backgrounds.

But the division of labor in Asia is not vertical either. What occurs between an industrialized country and a developing one with a supply of natural resources is, rather, a vertical division of labor where only certain sub-processes are passed to another country. This process is clearly visible when it becomes easy to find markets through the production process in various Asian countries.[10]

The pattern of international division of labor illustrated by the flying geese formation works, in Okita's view, because of the many differences in development stages, availability of natural resources, history, and culture among the Asian countries.

The model is not accepted universally, however. China is unhappy to see itself near the rear of the formation, especially a Japanese-led one. China would prefer to see itself as a very large bird supported by the geese.[11] This is particularly interesting, bearing in mind that the flying geese not only represent globalized production and industrial migration in Asia, but also the rapid growth of the regional economy.

Okita alone believed that the Asian nations, like the geese, would not continue soaring forever, and that the position of the countries within the formation would change if they managed to increase their technological capabilities. It was not only technological strength that mattered, but also infrastructure. Infrastructure was the key to increased technology. This included universities and high-tech research centers. Seen in this light, it would be very difficult for the formation to change.[12] This is why the "flying geese" illustration has gained recognition as the most suitable for explaining the dynamic rise of the Asian economies.

The Rise and Role of the Overseas Chinese Network

The "flying geese" phenomenon is appropriate for Asia, as long as no external factor needs to be considered.[13] As far as possible, there should be a conducive climate before dynamic economic development can take place. In addition to socioeconomic stability, the biggest factor to be considered is the fundamental state of the economy. This includes stable macroeconomic management, a high level of investment in "human capital" (especially education), a secure financial system, limited price distortion, and openness to foreign technology and trade within East Asia, all of which made Asia more attractive than other parts of the world.[14]

The result of these conducive policies led to the frenzied export of manufactured goods in the region. Paul Krugman, in his "It" theory, points out that the dynamic growth in Asia was equally the result of another external factor — information.[15] Pioneering companies provided admirable demonstrations to fellow companies of the endless possibilities for export of manufactured goods. This served to promote export-oriented policies and led to an increase in technological capabilities, giving these nations a comparative advantage.[16]

Krugman, however, could not refrain from asking (in a lecture to the World Bank) why this phenomenon occurred in Asia, rather than anywhere else, like Latin America. And what about China, which is located right next-door?

Accusing the World Bank of taking too much of a macroeconomic perspective, Gary Gereffi of Duke University takes the view that the answer to the riddle of Asia's dynamic growth lies in the micro-institutional foundations affecting economic development at a local level.[17] Furthermore, although other regions such as Latin America were blessed with similar comparative advantages such as low wages, the cultural differences between Latin America and Japan were more difficult to bridge than those between Japan and its Asian neighbors.[18] Asia also held a trump card: its long-established ethnic Chinese communities, which extend across the whole region and form an advanced economic and social network.

The presence of this network was one of the micro-institutional pillars of the development process, since it facilitated organizational innovations and technological learning at a domestic level, and transcended national and cultural differences. The network operated behind the scenes along well-established lines that had existed for decades — certainly long before the signing of agreements on regional cooperation made by regional forums such as the ASEAN Free Trade Agreement (AFTA) and Asia Pacific Economic Cooperation (APEC).

Despite their relatively small numbers, the overseas Chinese network has always played a significant role in shaping the economies of the Asian nations. Table 1.2 shows the population of ethnic Chinese in Southeast Asian countries as a percentage of each country's total population. Taking Southeast Asia as a whole, these figures show that ethnic Chinese, who make up only about 10% of the population, play a dominant role in the economies of Southeast Asia and Taiwan, as shown in Table 1.3.

	Total	Chinese	
Country	population[1]	population	% Chinese
Brunei	299,939	42,800	15.0
Cambodia	11,163,861	250,000[2]	2.0
Indonesia	209,774,138	5,244,353	2.5
Laos	5,116,959	66,520	1.3
Malaysia	20,491,303	6,147,391	30.0
Myanmar	46,821,943	8,193,840[2]	17.5
Philippines	76,103,564	1,522,071	2.0
Singapore	3,440,693	2,669,978	77.6
Taiwan	21,699,776	21,048,783	97.0
Thailand	59,450,818	8,323,115	14.0
Vietnam	75,123,880	1,051,734	1.4
Total	**529,086,894**	**54,560,585**	**10.3**

Table 1.2: Ethnic Chinese Population of Southeast Asia and Taiwan

Notes: [1] Figures are compiled from the US Census Bureau, World Population Estimates, and the East Asia Analytical Unit of the Australian Department of Foreign Affairs and Trade.
[2] Approximate figure only.

Sources: George T. Haley, Tan Chin Tiong, and Usha Haley, *New Asian Emperors* (Oxford: Butterworth-Heinemann, 1998); table compiled from *Far Eastern Economic Review*, February 26, 1998 and East Asia Analytical Unit estimates. Reproduced by permission of Butterworth-Heinemann Publishers, a division of Reed Educational & Professional Publishing Ltd.

In the Good Old Days
of the Asian Miracle

With special factors such as the overseas network on its side, East Asia grew far more rapidly than any other single region in the world. The World Bank even referred to a number of countries in the region as "high-performing Asian economies" (HPAEs) such as Japan.[19] Before the crisis hit, several Southeast Asian nations were recording phenomenal annual growth figures. Thailand, for example, enjoyed nearly a decade of worldwide acclaim as the world's fastest-growing economy. The country boasted moderate inflation, a stable exchange rate, seemingly healthy foreign exchange reserves, and a rapidly

Table 1.3: Economic Participation of the Overseas Chinese		
Country	Chinese as % of population	% of market capital controlled by Chinese
Brunei	15.0	[1]
Cambodia	2.0[3]	70.0[4]
Indonesia	2.5	73.0
Laos	1.3	[2]
Malaysia	30.0	69.0
Myanmar	17.5	[2]
Philippines	2.0	50–60.0
Singapore	77.6	81.0
Taiwan	97.0	95.0[5]
Thailand	14.0	81.0
Vietnam	1.4	45.0[6]

Notes: [1] In Brunei, ethnic Chinese often do not hold citizenship, and businesses are held in partnership with local citizens.
[2] Economies are currently moving away from strict socialist systems; figures still unavailable.
[3] Very rough estimates.
[4] Pre-Pol Pot figure.
[5] Percent of economy controlled by ethnic Chinese, not market capitalization.
[6] Estimate for Ho Chi Minh City only.

Sources: George T. Haley, Tan Chin Tiong, and Usha Haley, *New Asian Emperors* (Oxford: Butterworth-Heinemann, 1998); table compiled from *Far Eastern Economic Review*, February 26, 1998 and East Asia Analytical Unit estimates. Reproduced by permission of Butterworth-Heinemann Publishers, a division of Reed Educational & Professional Publishing Ltd.

declining incidence of absolute poverty. In short, Thailand's macroeconomy was in excellent shape. Because of this, the World Bank, the International Monetary Fund (IMF), and the United Nations Development Program (UNDP) regularly cited Thailand as a role model for other nations to follow.[20]

Other Asian countries were received with equal favor. Indonesia, a developing country with the world's fourth-largest population, and which had experienced hyperinflation of 650% in 1965, managed to maintain single-digit inflation for the next three decades. South Korea had begun to emulate Japan's success in the global markets, as was clearly visible by the number of South Korean products holding their own. South Korea was even admitted to the developed nations' club, the Organization for Economic Cooperation and Development

(OECD). Even communist China won praise for its impressive economic growth.

Such impressive achievements opened the doors to global investment in the region, which was supported by an abundance of natural resources and a large population enjoying steadily rising incomes. The region also had the endorsement of institutions such as the World Bank and the IMF, as well as of investment rating agencies such as Moody's and Standard & Poors.

What was the result of all this attention? Funding to Asia rose dramatically — more dramatically, in fact, than it should have. Coupled with the high level of investor confidence in the future of the region, Asia began to lose its grip on reality. The fantasy continued with the "Get on the 21st century bandwagon" scare-mongering tactics used toward global investors. Meanwhile, the overseas Chinese network continued to exert a degree of influence that could not be overlooked.

This network was not based on a clan or family system, but on simple trust.[21] The trust factor meant that financial caution was thrown to the wind. An example of the system at work may be seen in the US$260 million loan by Peregrine Investment Holdings to Steady Safe — an Indonesian company owned by a crony of the former president Soeharto — which was made without any paperwork being completed! Peregrine subsequently had great difficulty finding out what the money had been used for. As the local currency began to splutter, Peregrine, which had been a leading financial player in the region for a decade, was unable to keep up its efforts to minimize its losses, and eventually collapsed.[22]

Competitive Advantage:
A Forgotten Story of the Asian Miracle?

When the World Bank published its report entitled "The East Asian Miracle," it based its assessment on the growth in total factor productivity (TFP). According to the World Bank, TFP is calculated by subtracting from output growth the portion of growth due to capital accumulation, human capital accumulation, and labor force growth. TFP growth was determined using a production function estimated from cross-economy data. The result showed that six Southeast Asian nations — Hong Kong, Japan, South Korea, Thailand, Taiwan, and China — had reached a peak, while Malaysia, Singapore, and Indonesia had similar TFP growth rates to those of high-income economies. However, they were still ranked in the top third of all developing economies.[23]

Paul Krugman, however, in his controversial article, "The Myth of the Asian Miracle," ascertained that the so-called Asian miracle was not caused by TFP growth but by intensified application.[24] Phenomenal growth, rates posted by the Asian economies were achieved simply through the high rates of investment in the region and a high rate of growth of labor inputs given the increased labor participation in the region (see Table 1.4). Using data from a research paper presented by

Table 1.4: Paper Tigers				
	GDP per head*	GDP growth annual average %		
Country	1995, US$	1970–79	1980–89	1990–96
Hong Kong	23,900	9.2	7.5	5.0
Singapore	22,600	9.4	7.2	8.3
Taiwan	13,200	10.2	8.1	6.3
South Korea	11,900	9.3	8.0	7.7
Malaysia	10,400	8.0	5.7	8.8
Thailand	8,000	7.3	7.2	8.6
Indonesia	3,800	7.8	5.7	7.2
China	3,100	7.5	9.3	10.1
Philippines	2,800	6.1	1.8	2.8
Rich industrial countries	19,400	3.4	2.6	2.0

*At purchasing-power parity

Sources: Reproduced by permission of © The Economist, London, March 1, 1997. Table compiled from the IMF, ING Barings, and national statistics.

Alwyn Young, Krugman showed that very little TFP growth had actually occurred in Asia. He further suggested that mere increases in inputs, without an increase in the efficiency with which these inputs were used (investing in more machinery and infrastructure), would lead to diminishing returns.

Krugman chose Singapore to illustrate his idea of input-based growth. Between 1966 and 1990, the city-state's economy grew by a remarkable 8.5% per annum (three times as fast as the United States). However, Singapore's growth has been based largely on "one-time changes in behavior that cannot be repeated." Krugman argued that the doubling of the percentage of people employed in the past decades cannot continue forever. Furthermore, "a half-educated work force has been replaced by one in which the bulk of workers has high school diplomas; it is unlikely that a generation from now, most Singaporeans will have PhDs."[25] Based on this line of reasoning, a country that depends on high growth of inputs to fuel growth in economic output is unlikely to achieve future growth rates comparable to those of the past. Once inputs are exhausted and capital-to-output ratios rise toward rich-country levels, diminishing returns will set in and growth will slow sharply.

Krugman's views were highly criticized by others. An article in *The Economist* entitled "The Asian miracle: Is it over?,"[26] summarized these critics. First, many economists contend that Alwyn Young's calculations were wrong. In his work, Young looked at 118 countries between 1970 and 1985, and attempted to split GDP growth into the part that was attributable to increased inputs of labor and capital, and that which was attributable to more productive use of those inputs (which is, in essence, total factor productivity). The problem is that TFP growth is estimated as a residual — that is, the leftover that cannot be explained by increases in capital and labor.

Young's work is, therefore, subject to measurement problems, which helps to explain why other studies have produced higher estimates of productivity growth. For instance, Union Bank of Switzerland (UBS) repeated the same analysis using more up-to-date figures for 1970–90 and found that five East Asian countries (Hong Kong, Thailand, Singapore, South

Korea, and Taiwan) ranked in the top 12 (out of 104) for average TFP growth. In all five, productivity was roughly as important as investment in explaining growth. Michael Sarel of the IMF also found higher productivity growth in a study of ASEAN countries. He estimated that Singapore, Malaysia, and Thailand all had annual TFP growth of 2–2.5% between 1978 and 1996, compared with only 0.3% in the United States. He also found that TFP growth increased in most ASEAN countries between the 1980s and the 1990s.

Sarel also pointed out that Asian countries' TFP performance may have been even better, since it is hard for economists to distinguish between TFP growth and capital investment, because much technological progress and better ways to organize production are actually embodied in capital equipment imported from rich economies. As a result, the studies by UBS and the IMF may underestimate true productivity growth in high-investing Asian countries. In other words, some of the effects that Krugman dismissed as just capital investment growth may actually be productivity growth in another form.

Secondly, many people claim that Krugman under-estimated the significance of some of the changes he described. He tried to play down the notion of the Asian miracle by arguing that Asian countries merely invested a lot. Critics argue that Asia's ability to invest more effectively than other developing countries, and to import technology from the rest of the world, was itself an achievement. Investment in East Asia amounts to an average of 35% of GDP, almost twice as much as in Latin America.

Thirdly, Krugman has been criticized for being too quick to write off Asia's future prospects. The opportunity for catch-up remains immense, these critics say. In all of the Asian Tigers, the amount of capital per worker is considerably lower than in rich industrial economies. The average South Korean, for example, works with only two-fifths of the amount of capital available to his American counterpart. Furthermore, Asian workers' education could improve. In short, even if Krugman were right that most Asian growth had come from adding capital and labor, the limits to growth based on his diminishing return reasoning would still be a long way off.

Instead of taking Krugman's view, some economists in Asia at first attributed the slowdown in growth and exports (see Figure 1.2) to various cyclical, rather than structural, factors. These cyclical factors are, among others: (1) weak demand from rich countries; (2) the appreciation of the US dollar, to which many Asian currencies are in effect "linked"; and (3) the slump in the world semiconductor market in 1996 (affecting Singapore and South Korea). In essence, these proponents of the Asian economic development model defend themselves against Krugman's critics by saying that the Asian miracle is still very much alive and that there is nothing wrong with the model.

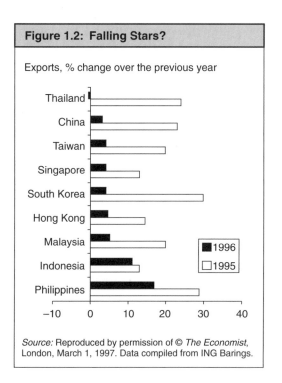

Figure 1.2: Falling Stars?

Exports, % change over the previous year

Source: Reproduced by permission of © *The Economist*, London, March 1, 1997. Data compiled from ING Barings.

The Demand for Democracy
and Political Openness

Increased economic prosperity tends to encourage more openness in political matters, as well as in economic matters. In China, the demand for political reform and democracy was linked to the economic prosperity that was spreading to all parts of Asia. The governments of Thailand and South Korea became more transparent when the military, which had hitherto held the reins of power, was forced to step down from the political stage. South Korea, while becoming more open politically, still refused to accept foreign products on its markets. Although Taiwan did not come under as much pressure to change as did China, Thailand, and South Korea, it decided to implement political reform and a democratic system if only to show its superiority in every respect over China. Interestingly, no such reforms took place in Singapore, which, as of mid-1999, had still not felt the need to implement any. The Philippines, on the other hand, whose economy was weaker than those of its neighbors, enjoyed the most open and democratic government in Asia.

Although these countries' economies were all experiencing dynamic economic growth, conditions varied considerably from country to country. The question, therefore, arose whether or not political reform should be implemented at all, and if so, when? Singapore, for instance, which had one of the most liberal economies in the region, did not see the need for democratization, since it felt it was more than capable of serving its people well. However, institutionalization outside politics had been progressing well. Supported by a government that believed it knew what was best for the nation and its people, Singapore had grown prosperous. However, it now discovered that political openness and democracy were becoming a necessity. Other countries such as Indonesia, South Korea, and Thailand, as well as Malaysia and China, had taken steps to yield to the demands for greater democracy, since their governments had little idea of what course of action to take.

In short, political and economic openness and institutionalization lost their relevance when the country and the government lost the ability to continue the process of modernization with the same degree of success as previously.

Financing the Development of Asia

One factor that played a major part in the phenomenal growth of Asia was the relatively short space of time between the beginning of the industrialization process and its successful conclusion. During this process, many East Asian countries were by no means inundated with cheap or abundant sources of funding. It was generally difficult for nations that had recently become independent to accumulate capital. Even their abundant natural wealth could not be relied upon.

Without sufficient funds, these countries had no choice but to rely on foreign loans for the development of their economies. Of course, since the state still exerted a strong influence, these foreign loans were initially dominated by government loans. Under these circumstances, the influx of foreign cash could still be controlled, and access to information about the origins of such loans, and when they were signed, was hard to come by. Another feature of these loans was the use to which they were put and the lack of accountability. In the end, though, it made little difference, since the amounts were small and processing times were long.

The situation began to change when many East Asian countries first started to record impressive and sustained macroeconomic performance, and at a time that coincided with the rise and growth of the private sector.[27] The new private companies began to secure their own foreign loans as an alternative way of financing the development of their business activities. The number of foreign loans secured privately grew rapidly. This resulted in the accumulation of global borrowed funds. Not surprisingly, therefore, the market for private loans became a buyer's market. This encouraged many banks and international financial institutions to provide loans to private companies throughout East Asia without conducting proper feasibility studies.[28] Accountability for the use of these funds was also largely disregarded. The dominant mood was one of blind faith in the future of the region's economy.

This buyer's market in private loans attracted not only foreign banks and the financial institutions, but local ones, too. The latter had no choice but to follow suit and disregard feasibility studies, although it should be admitted that, in several instances, they were actually forced by corrupt government officials to do so.[29] In contrast to the international banks and financing companies, local institutions lacked not only firm systems and procedures, but also clear and strong fund management structures. This naturally affected their ability to deal with non-performing loans, resulting in weaker supervision of operations within these institutions.

In truth, even before the crisis hit, many people had already become acutely aware of the vulnerability of the financial systems across East Asia, and this was a cause for some concern. But because of the predominant mood of overconfidence, triggered largely by this rapid and massive influx of global funds, such concerns were not taken seriously, and no effort was made to repair the individual countries' financial systems. Neither did investors or creditors appear to lose much sleep over the absence of proper bankruptcy laws across the region.[30] The financing model chosen for the development of the region was a time bomb. When the crisis hit, the bomb went off.

The Western School and the Asian School in the Asian Crisis

At a time when many people were openly admiring the Asian miracle, Paul Krugman was hesitant about that phrase in his article, "The Myth of the Asian Miracle." When his study was published in 1994, many Asians dismissed the work as an example of Western arrogance. They also dismissed the feeling among Western academics and experts that Asian countries needed to open up their markets and embrace the democratic tradition. These suggestions of the "Western School" of thought were not favorably received. Instead, many Asian leaders espoused the "Asian School" of thought, which promoted an Asian model of development and Asian values as more appropriate.

However, after Asia became embroiled in crisis, and the calls for open markets and democratization began to grow, Krugman's research gained widespread popularity. The Asian development model was suddenly blamed as the underlying cause of the crisis, as people began to understand just how flimsy its foundations had been. Not all people, of course, held this view. Those who did not believe in Krugman cited the fact that several countries in the region, despite their adherence to the Asian model and Asian values, were left unscathed.

It is clear that the crisis in Asia was not caused by the success of the Western School or the failure of the Eastern one. A study of ten Asian nations by Professor Linda Lim, who divided the countries into two groups — those heavily affected and those not so — showed that the former included some countries that had already begun to democratize, while the latter included several countries whose governments remained staunchly "undemocratic." These countries were members of the Asian Values School.

But the Asian Values School, which had been much admired prior to the Asian economic crisis, suddenly lost its credibility when the crisis hit during a period of unprecedented economic strength in the United States and economic recovery in Western Europe. The Asian miracle was particularly attacked for its reliance on "statist" industrial policy and cronyism (relationships between big businesses and the government), both of which contributed to moral hazards in the inefficient financial sector and the resultant over-investment in a classic asset bubble.

Professor Lim argued that there was no question that crony capitalism played a role in the over-inflation and subsequent deflation of economic growth and asset prices in Asia. However, she has also shown that the Western model of free-market-with-democracy contributed to Asia's plight as well.

First, she pointed out the "perils of openness." She argued that if openness was an essential ingredient of the Asian economic miracle, "too much openness too fast" was responsible for its downfall. She cited evidence such as the rapid and sweeping capital market liberalization that began in the late 1980s and led to a massive influx of foreign capital, which further contributed to the economic boom and the investment bubble of the 1990s. This influx of foreign funds, which in some cases amounted to as much as 75% of the equity capital on local stock markets, was a bigger problem, since domestic crony capitalism alone could not have fed a boom and created a bubble of such proportions. Open capital markets and capital account convertibility also increased these economies' vulnerability to currency speculation that could, at the appropriate moment, trigger a sudden massive exit of foreign funds as easily as these funds had previously entered. Furthermore, financial market liberalization in Asia also occurred before there were appropriate state or collective institutions to monitor and regulate financial institutions, or local expertise to manage them. Indonesia, for example, had more than 200 banks within a short time span and had inadequate experience in money management. With or without the moral hazard presented by local crony capitalism, the resultant excess supply of capital was bound to lead to some bad investments as capital started flowing into more marginal projects. Openness and the dominance of private enterprise in Asia also severely limited the governments' ability to intervene to control these flows.

Professor Lim also pointed out the "perils of democracy." Democracies that had taken hold in South Korea, Thailand, and the Philippines, caused a loss of government control over the macroeconomy since the late 1990s. Whereas previous authoritarian regimes could impose higher interest and taxation costs on local business communities almost at will, and had done so to maintain currency stability for decades, this became difficult with the increased political influence of business over elected legislatures whose members were either business-persons themselves, or required business support to get elected.

Thailand's short-lived coalition governments and frequent general elections made it particularly vulnerable to vested interest opposition to the fiscal and monetary contraction necessary to correct an internal imbalance.

By contrast, Hong Kong, which does not have an elected government, and Singapore, which has a parliament dominated by a single-party, have done relatively well through the economic crisis. Both administrations manage strong central economic control and can impose economic hardship on their populations or take stringent measures when necessary for economic stabilization. The Singapore government, for example, cooled off the domestic property market when it was still booming in 1996, and the Hong Kong government was able to ignore domestic business leaders' complaints about the currency peg hurting their businesses and raise local interest rates to protect the market against currency speculators in 1997. Proponents of the Western model, of course, do not see things this way. They constantly argue that it is the Asian parts of the Asian economic model that have failed, particularly statist industrial policy in South Korea and crony capitalism in Thailand, Malaysia, and Indonesia. They also blame the political management in the region, which ranges from the virtual absence of government in Thailand and authoritarianism in Indonesia, to a strong idiosyncratic leader in Malaysia.

From this analysis, Professor Lim concludes that neither of the two models is right. On the one hand, market openness, without the requisite institutional infrastructure and managerial expertise to manage it, can be a recipe for economic disaster, as indicated in the case of Indonesia and Thailand (see Figure 1.3). Even the normal workings of global financial markets themselves can be disruptive to small, open economies. Too much freedom too fast in both markets and politics can lead to a downfall, suggesting a continued need for a strong, benevolent, central state authority. On the other hand, statist industrial policy can lead to crony capitalism, excess capacity, over-leverage, and bad investment. Asian government involvement in industrial policy and the Asian cultural networks (*guanxi*) may also be indicted for fostering the crony

26

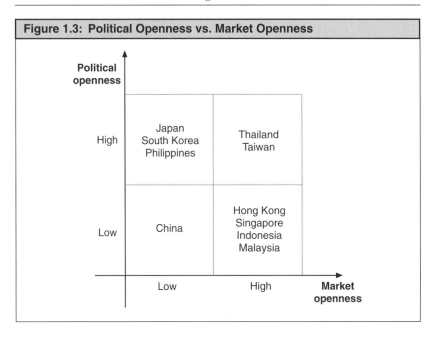

Figure 1.3: Political Openness vs. Market Openness

capitalism that led to over-investment in bad projects, such as Indonesia's Timor "national car" project and Malaysian's privatization of huge public infrastructure projects favoring politically well-connected businesses and individuals. (Michael Backman discusses these types of projects at length in his book, *Asian Eclipse*.[31]) In short, both the Western and Asian economic models have contributed not only to the Asian miracle, but also to the Asian meltdown. Instead of picking one model, Professor Lim stresses the importance of considering the country's particular configuration of historical, economic, political, social, and cultural forces to discern both the complex, multifaceted causes of the crisis and its eventual solutions.

The Asian Crisis: A Marketing Perspective

Each Asian country that succumbed to the crisis did so for reasons that were uniquely its own.[32] In order to gain a clear understanding of the Asian crisis, a wide-reaching framework is

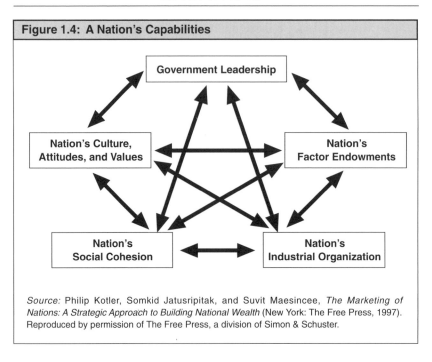

Figure 1.4: A Nation's Capabilities

Government Leadership

Nation's Culture, Attitudes, and Values

Nation's Factor Endowments

Nation's Social Cohesion

Nation's Industrial Organization

Source: Philip Kotler, Somkid Jatusripitak, and Suvit Maesincee, *The Marketing of Nations: A Strategic Approach to Building National Wealth* (New York: The Free Press, 1997). Reproduced by permission of The Free Press, a division of Simon & Schuster.

needed to analyze each country. One such framework has been developed by Philip Kotler, Somkid Jatusripitak, and Suvit Maesincee to assess the strengths and weaknesses of a particular country[33] (see Figure 1.4). The framework comprises five elements: government leadership; culture, attitudes, and values (CAV); factor endowments; social cohesion; and industrial organization. The strength of these five elements is critical in creating a country's "immunity" to a crisis.

The framework will be familiar to all those in the business of management, since it has analogies with a company's organization process. Government leadership is analogous with company management. CAV, along with factor endowments, represent the company's assets. Industrial organization and social cohesion are the company's enablers. From right to left, the matrix can be divided into two parts, with the right part representing economic aspects and the left representing social culture. This company-oriented matrix will be used in an attempt to understand why Asian countries were affected differently by the crisis.

Indonesia

Indonesia would never have been affected by the crisis, or at least would have recovered quickly, if it had been blessed with good leadership. It is not only long-term stability, but also managerial skills, that count. When the crisis first hit, the government was determined to take whatever steps were necessary. But its planning, organization, direction, and control left much to be desired. Despite the charisma he still had, Soeharto showed that he was no longer the visionary of old. He was undecided about the course of action to take. Soeharto's replacement, on the other hand, had plenty of vision, but lacked charisma, making it difficult for him to gain widespread support for his proposals. Abdurrahman Wahid, the recently elected president, should bring back many of these supports from various institutions. The return of confidence in the country, however, must be supported by the government's commitment to, and decisive action in bringing about, the long-awaited fundamental political and economic reforms.

Despite scoring high on factor endowments, Indonesia is very weak in the other four elements. This has placed a heavy burden on the nation's ability to deal with the crisis.

Thailand

Sociopolitically speaking, prior to the crisis, Thailand was stable. It was (and continues to be) ruled by a monarch who is universally respected. Unlike Indonesia, it had no problems with social cohesion, CAV, or industrial organization. But because of its frequent changes, the government was unable to build up a strong basis of support and therefore, found it difficult to implement the necessary course of action. It is not surprising that Thailand fell victim to the crisis.

South Korea

South Korea has no abundance of resources, but it enjoys good social cohesion, since it is made up of a single ethnic group with a strong industrial organization. But because of its weak government leadership and CAV, this industrial organization was developed with no thought for efficiency or effectiveness. Under normal circumstances, this could be tolerated. But in a period of crisis, it only made things worse.

The Philippines

The Philippines is one of the most democratic countries in Asia; its government leadership should not have resembled the lottery that it does. Although it has had a good succession system in place, this system has not been able to guarantee a visionary leader — something that the Philippines, which lagged behind its neighbors in the frenzy of development, desperately needed to help bring the country up to speed.

The Philippines still faces the problem of factor endowments and industrial organization, as well as scoring low marks for CAV. If it has one thing going for it, it is the fact that it has had a democratically elected government. This has contributed greatly to the nation's social cohesion.

Malaysia

A charismatic and visionary leader does not always have to make the right moves all the time; only when it really matters. This is the story of Malaysia (see Box 1.1). Although potential problems loomed in its social cohesion and industrial organization, it was able to employ strong government leadership to optimize its CAV and endowment factors, thereby minimizing the negative effects of the crisis.

Box 1.1

The Myth and Reality of Malaysia's Capital Controls

With his recent electoral triumph and his political integrity under increasing scrutiny at home and abroad as 1999 drew to a close, Malaysia's Prime Minister Dr. Mahathir Mohammad responded enthusiastically to opportunities to talk up his unique and controversial approach to addressing the impact of Asia's financial crisis. He was saying, in effect, that he was right earlier, when everyone said he was wrong — except for maybe MIT economist Paul Krugman — and he was still right when he says he knows what's best for Malaysia.

And in fact, Dr. Mahathir was getting some newfound respect in influential circles for his argument that capital controls saved Malaysia from the severe social and financial upheaval that its neighbors experienced. Even formerly harsh critics were heard admitting that while capital controls might not have helped as much as Dr. Mahathir would like observers to believe, these controls did not hurt as much as many analysts believed they would.

This perception was extremely dangerous for Asia, and bodes ill for Asia's chances of avoiding a future financial panic. Benign acceptance of the notion that capital controls may be all right after all, is nestled in the too-easy assumption that what was wrong with Malaysia — and, indeed, Asia — had been fixed. But it hadn't.

First, consider the impact of Dr. Mahathir's capital controls and why they did not cause the upheaval that detractors warned would take place. In fact, capital controls had almost no impact, either to benefit or damage Malaysia's economy, because they were imposed when they no longer mattered. By mid-1998, Asia had fallen as far it was going to economically. The task was no longer to break the fall, but to manage recovery.

And that, in fact, was Dr. Mahathir's dilemma, and the point where he and his former protégé and deputy prime minister, Anwar Ibrahim, finally and irrevocably parted ways. Real recovery — which would safeguard the economy from similar future shocks — would require the fundamental remaking of Malaysia's corporate and financial sectors. For Dr. Mahathir, that price was just too great politically. Indeed, it would have demanded the dismantling of much of what Dr. Mahathir considered his life's work. But to less-involved observers, creative destruction was required to move Malaysia forward under significantly different conditions than before.

So, capital controls were less of a financial strategy to save Malaysia's economy than they were a political ploy to preserve it. Indeed, and despite the much-hyped current banking sector reform, Malaysia has emerged from Asia's meltdown pretty much the same — and worse in terms of the restructuring of politically connected corporations — as it was: (1) Domestic enterprise is dominated by poorly managed, politically connected conglomerates; (2) Enterprise is overwhelmingly financed with debt; and (3) There is little pressure for transparency, and therefore little accountability to shareholders.

As a result, Malaysia is, unlike its neighbors that have pursued painful reforms and forced large-scale corporate restructuring, just as vulnerable to the next panic-driven crisis as it was to this one.

If that sounds overly pessimistic, consider for a moment the corporate, banking, and political landscapes in Malaysia compared to that of its neighbors. Although Indonesia is an extreme exception, Japan, South Korea, and Thailand have all pressured large, uncompetitive conglomerates to slim down, to focus on core businesses, and to boost productivity and efficiency. (Indonesia's conglomerates have had even less choice.)

In Malaysia, the most hopeless corporations have been

saved by acquisition by public sector corporations with taxpayers footing the bill, or have been permitted to merge with or be acquired by less-distressed affiliates in deals that diluted and obliterated minority shareholders' interests. They have also received additional debt financing that they clearly don't deserve. Most real restructuring in Malaysia has taken place below the horizon, among corporations that are too small to appear on Dr. Mahathir's radar screen, and, therefore, unlikely to benefit from government benevolence. In that, they are probably fortunate.

Banking sector reform appears to be driven by the notion — akin to Dr. Mahathir's notion for the corporate sector — that big equals good. Well, maybe, but reforming the regulatory environment should take precedence. Yet, reforms are taking second — a deep second — place to refinancing (rather than restructuring) corporate debt, "encouraging" banks to continue lending to sickly firms, and forcing the banks themselves into what initially turned out to be a poorly thought-out plan to force consolidation in the sector.

Dr. Mahathir ultimately admitted that the initial merger plan had "no logic" and was "arbitrary," and it was eventually scrapped, in large part due to pressure from ethnic Chinese bankers who felt they were being treated unfairly, and whose political support had grown dramatically in importance to Dr. Mahathir. A new merger plan — providing for ten main banking groups rather than the six first proposed — was announced in February 2000.

Meanwhile, Malaysia's neighbors pursued reforms that Dr. Mahathir chose to scoff at, including up to 100% foreign ownership of distressed banks.

In both the corporate and banking instances, the lack of transparent corporate governance, adequate accounting practices, and bankruptcy provisions overseen by a judiciary trained to do so, will mean that Malaysia will have little alternative to debt financing, because it will be unable to restore investor trust in underlying corporate values necessary to develop its capital market. Whatever one argues about capital controls, they certainly did not instill international confidence in Malaysian equities, and although key index funds had announced that Malaysian stocks would be reintroduced by the end of 1999, foreign investors showed little interest in plowing in new money. Fund managers seemed resigned — "I don't want to, because I don't like it, but my job is to beat the index,"[34] one said — but were clearly unenthusiastic. Meanwhile, local investors were back to borrowing to invest in early 2000, and accounted for recent share price gains.

The bottom line was this: the government might have preserved Malaysia, Inc., but the clock was still ticking.

Hong Kong

A government composed of experienced people should have been quicker to react to the economic downturn. But because of the lack of charisma and vision within its top ranks, the Hong Kong government could not perform to the best of its ability. What Hong Kong lacked in factor endowments, it made up in industrial organization, CAV, and social cohesion. However, the city-state's government leadership now caused its CAV to move in unwelcome directions. The characteristics that made Hong Kong so fundamentally strong were not enough to save it from the crisis.

Taiwan

Taiwan is the best example of a nation that successfully "beat" the crisis. It enjoyed strong government leadership. Born out of the democratic process, it had a visionary and charismatic president. It was well institutionalized. The government found it easy to manage the nation's CAV, both before and after the crisis. In addition, with social cohesion, industrial organization, and factor endowments similar to those of Hong Kong, it is no surprise that Taiwan was in such a healthy state.

Singapore

Singapore has one of the most liberal economies in the world. Politically, it was (and still is) governed by an authoritarian regime. In spite of this, it was institutionalized — except politically. This encouraged the government to continue to modernize. This kind of government leadership, although essentially non-democratic, had an influence on national CAV and even added to social cohesion.

This, in turn, meant that the lack of factor endowments did not present a major problem for Singapore, since it had a strong industrial organization that extended even to neighboring countries that had the advantage of endowments. Clearly, then, the Asian crisis had no major adverse effect on Singapore. It was well prepared for such an eventuality.

China

Prior to the crisis, China's situation was similar to that of Singapore — a rapidly developing economy with a stagnant, authoritarian government. This was not of its own choosing. China, the most populous nation on earth, had a serious social cohesion problem, and an underdeveloped CAV and industrial organization. Therefore, although it had factor endowments, it still needed to pay close attention to the rapidly developing world around it.

China's government, however, has shown several signs of transition toward democracy. Moreover, the country now appears to be reasonably "well-governed," having succeeded in raising the level of prosperity and begun to modernize. This can be clearly seen from China's impending entry into the World Trade Organization (WTO), which will not only accelerate trade liberalization, but also symbolize its gradual progression toward a more "democratic" country.

Japan

The government leaders of Japan frequently change. But the number and names of government departments do not, so the frequent governmental changes does the country little harm.

What did harm Japan, however, was the lack of an authoritative government capable of taking the difficult steps that were needed during the crisis, despite widespread support for them. Essentially, it was the debt-of-honor factor, which meant that Japan's leaders were unable to manage the nation's CAV effectively in times of difficulty. However, the country had a level of social cohesion and industrial organization that any country would be proud of. Ultimately, this is the reason why, in spite of poor natural endowments, Japan still did not need to worry during times of hardship.

What's Next?

As Asia continues to sift through the wreckage of one of the greatest crises since World War II, Asians must come to accept that the old Asian miracle days are over. Both Asian countries and companies must undergo the needed, but painful, reforms. In our view, the old "Asia" brand of high growth, *guanxi*, and state-led development have crumbled. The Asian crisis has shown the world that such high growth rates are not sustainable, because they were not substantiated by sound investments, good governance, and strong economic fundamentals. In short, Asia was a "bubble."

What Asia has to do now is to reposition its old "bubble" brand image into a "sustainable" one. This will not be an easy job and will require everyone's concerted participation. Asia must "unlearn" its old habits and "relearn" new ways of building sustainable economies. However, while we recommend that Asia changes, we also acknowledge that it must adopt these changes gradually. Referring back to Professor Lim's view, we believe that rebuilding Asia should be just like treating a severe drug addict. We cannot just immediately stop supplying the drugs. Instead, we should lessen the dosage gradually. Otherwise, we may risk the patient dying. Everyone is now aware of Asia's dark side and bad old habits (explained in great detail in Michael Backman's *Asian Eclipse*). These habits must be changed; but they cannot be transformed within a short period of time. If changes happen too quickly, Asians may face the "perils of democracy and openness," as described earlier by Professor Lim.

A successful repositioning effort requires not only promoting the new brand, but also a strong commitment to and, more importantly, implementation of fundamental reforms. Promoting the brand is only a promise, but a promise must be fulfilled by real and accountable actions. The repositioning efforts need to be taken at both the country and company levels. Thus, Part II of this book covers how Asia can once again become one of the most attractive regions in the world. Part III will then give strategic guidelines aimed at assisting companies in Asia to survive, or even to emerge from the crisis as winners.

---

1 Todd Crowell and Robin Ajello, "Cheers and tears," *Asiaweek*, July 11, 1997.

2 Statement by Singapore prime minister, Goh Chok Tong.

3 Jim Erickson, "Battle over Asia's money," *Asiaweek*, July 18, 1997, p. 32.

4 Ibid.

5 Supporting data and information on the Asian crisis chronology was gathered from the Asian crisis chronology section of Nouriel Roubini's Asian crisis website (http://www.stern.nyu.edu/~nroubini/asia/AsiaHomepage.html) and *Asiaweek*'s Asian crisis chronology summary, "The evolution of a crisis," July 17, 1998.

6 Linda Lim, "Who's 'Model' Failed? Implications of the Asian Economic Crisis," *The Washington Quarterly*, Vol. 23, No. 3 (1998).

7 Philip Kotler, Somkid Jatusripitak, and Suvit Maesincee, *The Marketing of Nations: A Strategic Approach to Building National Wealth* (New York: The Free Press, 1997).

8 Hadi Soesastro, "Teknologi dan Keunggulan Komparatif (Technology and Comparative Advantage)," in M. Arsyad Anwar, The Kian Wee, and Iwan Jaya Aziz (eds.), *Pemikiran, Pelaksanaan Dan Perintisan Pembangunan Ekonomi* (Jakarta: Gramedia Pustaka Utama, 1992), p. 547, with reference to Kaname Akamasu,

"A historical pattern of economic growth in developing countries," *The Developing Economies*, No. 1 (1962).

9 Ibid., p. 547, with reference to Saburo Okita, "Prospect of the Pacific economies," presented to the Pacific Economic Cooperation Conference — Issues and Opportunities, Report of the Fourth Pacific Economic Cooperation Conference, Seoul, April 29–May 1, 1985 (Seoul: South Korea Development Institute, June 1985), pp. 18–29.

10 "Flying Geese: An Unequal Alliance in Asia," in Walter Hatch and Kozo Yamamura (eds.), *Asia in Japan's Embrace: Building Regional Production Alliances* (Cambridge, UK: Cambridge University Press, 1996).

11 Hadi Soesastro, "Teknologi dan Keunggulan Komparatif (Technology and Comparative Advantage)," op. cit., p. 549, with reference to Edward K.Y. Chen, "Hong Kong's role in Asian and Pacific economic development," *Asia Development Review*, Vol. 7, No. 2 (1989), p. 35.

12 See Edward Nielsen, "Asian Silicon Valley fails," *The Jakarta Post*, April 19, 1999. The article illustrates the many obstacles facing the process of technological development.

13 Hadi Soesastro, "Teknologi dan Keunggulan Komparatif (Technology and Comparative Advantage)," op. cit., p. 547, with reference to "*Angsa-Angsa Terbang di atas Pasifik* (Flying Geese Over the Pacific)," by noted economist and former Economic Minister M. Saidi, *Tempo*, June 4, 1988.

14 World Bank, *The East Asian Miracle: World Bank Policy Research Report* (Oxford: Oxford University Press, 1993), p. 7.

15 Paul Krugman, "Technology and Changing Comparative Advantage in the Pacific Region," in Hadi Soesastro and Mari Pangestu (eds.), *Technological Challenge in the Asia-Pacific Economy* (Sydney: Allen & Unwin, 1990).

16 Hadi Soesastro, "Teknologi dan Keunggulan Komparatif (Technology and Comparative Advantage)," op. cit., p. 550, with reference to Paul Krugman, "Technology and Changing Comparative Advantage in the Pacific Region," in Hadi Soesastro and Mari E. Pangestu (eds.), *Technological Challenge in the Asia-Pacific Economy*, op. cit.

17 Gary Gereffi, "Commodity Chains and Regional Divisions of Labor," in Eun Mee Kim (ed.), *The Four Asian Tigers: Economic Development and the Global Political Economy* (San Diego, California: San Diego Academic Press), p. 97.

18 Ibid.

19 See World Bank, *The East Asian Miracle*, op. cit.

20 Peter G. Warr, "Thailand," in Ross H. McCleod and Ross Garnaut (eds.), *East Asia in Crisis: From Being a Miracle to Needing One* (London: Routledge, 1998), p. 49.

21 George T. Haley, Chin Tion Tan, and Usha C.V. Haley, *New Asian Emperors: The Overseas Chinese, Their Strategies, and Competitive Advantage* (Oxford: Butterworth-Heinemann, 1998), p. 13.

22 Ibid.

23 World Bank, *The East Asian Miracle*, op. cit., p. 54.

24 Paul Krugman, "The myth of the Asian miracle," *Foreign Affairs*, November–December 1994, pp. 62–78.

25 Ibid.

26 This section draws heavily on "The Asian miracle: Is it over?," *The Economist*, March 1, 1997. Summarized by permission of © *The Economist*, London.

27   Paul Krugman, *The Return of Depression Economics* (London: Allen Lane The Penguin Press, 1999), p. 85.
28   Ibid., p. 88.
29   Ibid.
30   Michael Backman, *Asian Eclipse: Exposing the Dark Side of Business in Asia* (Singapore: John Wiley & Sons, 1999), p. 24.
31   Ibid.
32   Ross Garnaut, "The East Asian Crisis," in McCleod and Garnaut (eds.), *East Asia in Crisis*, op. cit., p. 7.
33   Kotler et al., *The Marketing of Nations*, op. cit., p. 112.
34   McBride, Sarah, "Fund managers in Asia re-evaluate weightings," *The Wall Street Journal Interactive*, February 24, 2000, Internet edition.

PART
II

Transforming
the Nations

CHAPTER 2

IN SEARCH OF THE SUSTAINABLE ECONOMY

Even before the outbreak of Asia's economic crisis in mid-1997, there were signs in 1995–96 that Asia would undergo difficulties.[1] The GDP growth rate and export growth in a number of Asian countries such as Thailand and South Korea had begun to show quite a significant decline.[2]

A decline in performance appeared in almost every country in East Asia, as shown by macroeconomic indicators between 1990 and 1997.[3] Between 1990 and 1995, declining performance was already visible, although on average the macroeconomic performance rate in this region was still higher than those in other regions in the world.

Unfortunately, at that time, this decline was not seen as a signal for alarm. Even an article by Paul Krugman that appeared in *Foreign Affairs* a year earlier, if commented on at all, produced mostly defensive responses. Very few people took Krugman's comments as a warning.[4] Likewise, when a number of companies in South Korea and Thailand began to be financially strapped in servicing their offshore loans in early 1997, few took this as a sign of danger.[5] This failure to perceive the true situation in the region could be attributed to overconfidence in the future of Asia and the Pacific in the 21st century, but it could also have been the result of the focus at the time being on the future of Hong Kong after the handing over of its sovereignty from Britain to China.

Therefore, not much had been done in the way of adjustment.[6] Most countries in East Asia did not want to budge from their winning strategy. Corruption was not seen as a flaw that could incapacitate East Asia's ability to maintain its high performance level.[7] However, when the crisis began to be felt and its magnitude was discerned, there was an awareness that what had seemed a winning strategy was no longer appropriate, particularly given the increasingly impressive economic performance being achieved by North America and Western Europe.

The countries in Asia finally realized that unless drastic adjustments were undertaken, they would fall behind countries in other regions in the world, especially in their ability to attract investment. The crisis that emerged in mid-1997 provided a momentum for regional renewal, in the same way that an organization or a company generally begins to realize the need for change only after experiencing a crisis. This renewal process at the national level can be illustrated with the case of the United States (see Box 2.1). Yet, the uniqueness of each country in the economic, social, and political sectors would affect its process of renewal. Unlike the European Union, East Asia does not have a strong unifying bond. Neither does it have a charismatic figure or an authority that can initiate or lead a renewal. These factors would certainly affect the harmonization of Asian renewal.

Box 2.1

Country Renewal: The United States' Experience

When Asia was first hit by the crisis, many people suspected that sooner or later the effects would spread to the US economy, particularly when considering that a number of major US companies had made East Asia one of the main markets for their products. In October 1997, stocks on the New York Stock Exchange went bearish and

---

44

the share price index fell. Yet, within a short span of time, the index returned to its normal position and even moved upward. In short, the US economy had not been affected much by the Asian crisis.

The same worries arose when the Russian crisis began in mid-1998.[8] The New York Stock Exchange was jolted, but then became calm again and moved upward.[9] The impressive economic performance of the United States continued. In line with the signs of Asia's economic recovery, the Dow Jones index continued to move up. It reached a peak on March 29, 1999 when the index rose to the historic high level of 10,000.[10] This achievement signified high optimism in the strength and future of the US economy.

This achievement is in contrast to the condition of the US economy in the second half of the 1980s. US companies seemed helpless against Japanese companies that had developed high-quality products at affordable prices. Ironically, these companies' success was due in part to their having learned about the importance of quality management and marketing from American experts such as W.E. Deming, Peter Drucker, and Philip Kotler.

At first, the US government and companies attempted to adopt a political approach to overcome the declining trend in US economic performance and the growing US trade deficit with Japan. Even when Yasuhiro Nakasone became Japan's prime minister in 1986, he agreed to launch a campaign calling upon the Japanese to buy foreign, particularly American, products. This effort, however, was not successful. So US companies moved in another direction; they started to study Japanese methodologies, such as total quality management, just-in-time production, and team-based decision-making.

Nevertheless, these efforts did not immediately bear fruit. For this reason, when Bill Clinton campaigned for the US presidency in 1992, he emphasized economic development that would improve the capability of US companies and would open new markets for US products. When Clinton became president, he applied pro-business anti-trust and fair competition policies and the enforcement of intellectual property rights. To create new markets for US products, he called for regional and multilateral cooperation and liberalization of world trade.

Through these efforts, US companies slowly developed the capacity to compete globally. The US economy started on the renewal path. After passing through a crisis in the second half of the 1980s, the United States successfully carried out its renewal process, through a combination of government leadership, endowments, positive CAV, social cohesion, and industrial organization.[11] This experience of the United States of emerging from a crisis should be adopted as a model by Asian countries.

The sustainability model, which is an organizational change model, will be adopted to depict and analyze Asia's development and renewal process. The following section will dwell on what the model is like, why it is adopted, and how to use it in the analysis.

The Sustainability Model

In *Crisis & Renewal*, David Hurst explained that organizational renewal is "not a one-shot affair but an ongoing process — a continual struggle."[12] An organization, whether a company or a nation, must never be complacent about what it has accomplished; it must continually adjust to the changing "market." To illustrate, Hurst developed a model of continuous organizational change and renewal (see Figure 2.1). The model consists of two intersecting loops that form an infinity symbol. The first loop (with the solid line) represents the process of growth, while the second loop (the reverse "S" with dotted line) represents the process of renewal.

46

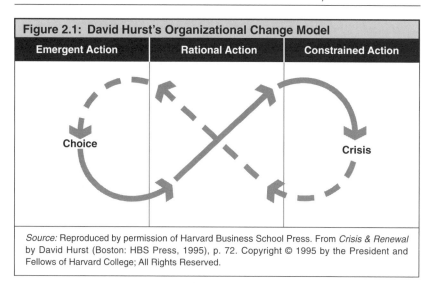

Figure 2.1: David Hurst's Organizational Change Model

Emergent Action	Rational Action	Constrained Action

Choice

Crisis

We added several elements to David Hurst's loop (see Figure 2.2) to explain the "change journey." The first loop is named the "performing cycle," while the second loop is named the "transforming cycle." We will begin the "journey" with the performing cycle. When a new organization is first established, the organization is usually in the "emergent" phase (1). Activities are action-oriented rather than deliberate, as everyone within the organization is enthusiastic and highly motivated, and strategy tends to be emergent rather than planned. In this start-up stage, a strong leadership is generally assumed by an entrepreneur who sets a clear vision and "exploits" the organization's energy, resources, and people in order to realize it (2). In this stage, typically, a good management system is not yet put in place.

If efforts in the early stages succeed, the organization will enter the "rational" phase. In this phase, it will normally experience significant growth in performance, accompanied by a steady increase in scale. As a result, people within the organization become confident in their choices. As the growing business requires better control, a formal management system is put in place. Unlike the "emergent" phase, a bureaucracy is formed and everyone has a clear job description. When the

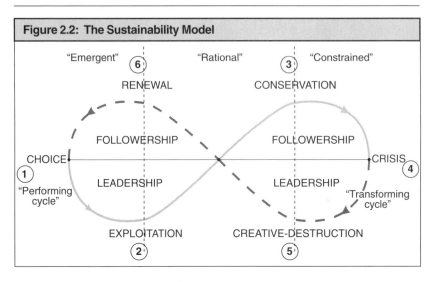

Figure 2.2: The Sustainability Model

business has become large in scale and scope, the leader will likely have lost touch with the rank-and-file and become less sensitive to the marketplace. Good "followership" is thus necessary. The followers must sense the changing market, analyze it, and report their assessments to the leader.

When the management system is fully operationalized, organizations often become over-bureaucratized and bent on "conserving" their systems (3). This stage is dangerous, as the whole organization becomes "a prisoner of its own system." It becomes "constrained" by the very systems it has put in place. The danger is that the company's good internal management system may not fit well with the changing "new market" and environment. This is when a "crisis" usually occurs and where the "performing cycle" ends (4).

When the crisis strikes, an organization needs to enter the "transforming cycle" by going through major restructuring efforts to adapt to the "new market" and environment. It is even better when the organization creates a "sense of crisis" and undertakes "creative destruction" before the real crisis occurs (5). Jack Welch at General Electric (GE) created a "sense of crisis" while the US conglomerate was still financially strong. He undertook "creative destruction" by selling several GE subsidiaries that had failed to achieve a number one or two position in their markets. In the creative destruction stage, an unpopular decision is often needed to start the "transforming cycle." Very often, the business must bring in an outsider — sometimes someone from outside the industry — to be the transformation leader.

In "renewing" the company, the transformation leader must enforce changes (6). The task is to destroy the "existing-unfit" values and practices and to create the "future-hopeful-fit" values and practices. In this stage, the organization once again needs good followership. The leader must gain followers if he or she is to succeed in launching a new, successful performing cycle. One infinity loop ends, but the second loop then starts. The key lesson here is that an organization must never be satisfied with its accomplishments. Instead, it must continually adjust itself to the changing environment.

Although the sustainability model is essentially a management model, it can be used to describe Asia's development, as well as to pinpoint the need for an Asian renewal. It can give better insights into what Asia has done and how it must proceed to rebuild itself from the debilitating crisis.

The Growth Phase of Asian Development

In this section, we will apply the performing cycle phase of the sustainability model to describe Asia's development or growth process, which comprises three stages: the emergent stage, the rational stage, and the constrained stage (see Figure 2.3).

The Emergent Stage

Compared with Western European, North American, or even South American economies, Asian economies are relatively young. Except for Japan and Thailand, most Asian countries were previously subjected to colonization (also undertaken by Japan) until World War II. After the war, a number of countries in Asia began to establish nation-states.

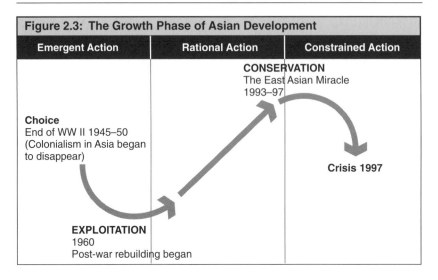

Figure 2.3: The Growth Phase of Asian Development

In most countries, the process of becoming a nation-state did not unfold smoothly. Apart from disturbances exerted by the colonizing countries, a number of nation-states experienced difficulty in pooling their past collective memories. In a number of countries this process took quite a long time. Sometimes it was interrupted by armed rebellions, which also lasted for a long time. As a result, the process of economic development and the preparation of the infrastructure such as education and laws, needed for economic development, became somewhat neglected.

Besides, the Cold War between the capitalist camp led by the United States and the communist camp under the Soviet Union, and also the People's Republic of China, had made the Asian region an arena of rivalry, a factor that retarded the process of economic development. In short, many countries in Asia had to prioritize political matters over economic ones until as late as the early 1960s. On the other hand, the "flying geese" phenomenon is considered by many commentators to be one of the factors triggering dynamic economic development in East Asia. This is also supported by the fact that the region's transformation from an agricultural economy to an industrial economy had been rapid.

To most East Asian countries, an agricultural economy was

inevitable. Land was quite fertile and crops were easily grown. Only a small number of skilled and highly educated workers and funds would be needed in such a situation. To most young East Asian countries, this low demand for physical and human capital enabled them to easily undertake their economic development.

However, the agricultural economy was traditional in nature, in that production was focused only on commodities without much effort to generate added value. Therefore, the return generated from this agricultural economy was not high, although it became the basis for the build-up of savings and human capital improvement.

These factors assumed a great significance when Japan, whose industry had risen again, began to look for new markets and new low-cost manufacturing bases. In addition to Japan's close proximity, a number of East Asian countries were former Japanese colonies. They were once Japan's low-cost manufacturing bases for its "old" industries and could therefore learn fast from Japan. South Korea and Taiwan were two such countries. South Korea has even copied Japan's economic development strategy, particularly in the manufact-uring sector.

In 1961, South Korea was led by General Park Chung Hee, an authoritarian but visionary leader.[13] South Korea, not as rich in natural resources as other East Asian countries, recognized that it could survive and grow if its manufacturing products could be sold in the global market. Gen. Park looked to Japan as the model. Through what was known as "Japan Inc.," the Japanese government had led Japanese companies to enter industries generating manufacturing products needed in the world market. Furthermore, the Japanese government protected the domestic market, although this led to strong competition in the domestic market among Japanese companies. The Japanese government maintained the inflation rate at a very low level (almost 0%), but bolstered savings so that the financial resources for industrialization became easily and cheaply available. Resources were made even more possible by *keiretsu*, where companies belonging to one group or affiliation helped one another in financial and marketing matters.

Being a new country, and having fought a war as part of the Cold War, South Korea clearly did not have as many resources and infrastructures as Japan. Luckily, in the 1960s, South Korea, along with Taiwan, assumed a strategic geopolitical significance. The United States, as the leader of the capitalist states, wanted to see these two countries become models for other developing nations.[14] Hence, the United States fully supported the process of industrial development in South Korea, providing capital and technological assistance. It even tolerated Gen. Park's militaristic and authoritarian administration for the sake of developing South Korea as a model.

In his state-led development strategy, Gen. Park later introduced the concept of *chaebol*, a business group dealing in a particular line of industry. Gen. Park's administration also fully supported the provision of funds and protection against competition. Even the domestic market was protected. In the meantime, to make the *chaebol* highly competitive, the government sought to maintain a low rate of workers' wages. In this way, a *chaebol* could be a low-cost producer able to sell its products widely in the international market.[15]

The success stories of "Japan Inc." and "Korea Inc." inspired many East Asian governments, generally authoritarian, to adopt the state-led development strategy involving such steps as shifting from an agricultural economy to an industrial economy, providing full financial and domestic protection support to the industrial "pioneers" and to the creation of *kaishas* or *chaebols*.

The Rational Stage

One of the main objections that was raised to the "flying geese" phenomenon was its being Japan-centric or Japanese-dominant. To a number of East Asian countries, this was a major problem, owing to Japan's oppressive treatment of them during the Japanese occupation. China and other countries objected to the view of Japanese leadership. Yet, Japanese companies managed to locate factories, and even the companies supporting these factories, from banks to trading companies, in East Asia.

This process took place over quite a long time, in which there were seemingly few competitors. Some US companies operated widely in East Asia, but not as part of their international labor division pattern. The same was true of the overseas Chinese, who constitute one of the engines of dynamic development in East Asia. Besides, compared with the Japanese, the overseas Chinese were rather late in undertaking industrialization. It was only later that they followed the rhythm of Japan's international labor division pattern.

Malaysia felt it necessary to run its "Look to the East" policy when Dr. Mahathir Mohammad came to power in 1981. Other East Asian countries, such as South Korea and Indonesia, nurtured a wish to copy the concept of Japan Inc. after seeing how Japanese companies controlled the international market. These Japanese companies had by then defeated American and European companies. Many East Asian governments hoped to establish a ministry in imitation of Japan's Ministry of International Trade and Industry (MITI), which played a central role in Japan Inc. In short, Japan's success in the economic field made many Asian countries look up to it as their model.

Taking these steps, the East Asian countries gradually emerged as industrialized countries. In the late 1980s, four East Asian countries — South Korea, Taiwan, Hong Kong, and Singapore — emerged as newly industrialized countries (NICs). China would soon follow suit, as would Indonesia, Malaysia, Thailand, and the Philippines, which many had considered the next NICs. They not only became industrialized countries, but also showed impressive performance and registered a high growth rate over a long period.

As for Singapore, Hong Kong, and Taiwan, their governments had practiced transparency and fairness, resulting in these economies enjoying a strong competitive edge and a high rate of performance. In the case of a number of other East Asian countries that adopted the state-led development strategy along with economic and political distortions, their performance levels did not reflect their real capabilities. These countries could not compete in a condition where transparency and fairness were the prime factors. However, as they continued to enjoy a large-scale global capital inflow, their pseudo-competitiveness did not seem quite a problem. Instead, it even contributed substantially to the export boom that prevailed in Asia in 1995.

It is clear, however, that the countries that had first become NICs, or that were in the frontline of the "flying geese" formation, were those that had enjoyed political stability earlier than other Asian countries. Unfortunately, this was achieved, and then maintained, under an authoritarian system. As a result, economic development could take place rapidly but was enveloped with economic and political distortions.[16]

The Constrained Stage

Prior to the outbreak of the crisis, there was concern that, in many respects, the process of economic development in Asia was not coupled with political development such as democratization, freedom of assembly and of expression, and respect for human rights. A number of Asian leaders hid behind the notion of "Asian values,"[17] a pretext that Asia has its own concept and ways of developing its economic and political sectors. As there was then no strong evidence that these Asian values were "burdensome" to the process of economic development, they were considered the winning strategy and, as such, should be maintained regardless of the prevalence of economic and political distortions. When Asia began to undergo a decline in macroeconomic stability, confidence in Asian values and Asia's economic future eroded quickly. A revival of this confidence rests on the promotion of transparency and fairness — in other words, on scrapping economic and political distortions. This is not an impossible task. What counts is that revisions to the old model enable the East Asian countries to respond to such demands as mandate, competence, transparency, and fairness (see Box 2.2).

Box 2.2

The Asian Sustainability Model: Three Success Stories

Three Asian countries — Singapore, Hong Kong, and Taiwan — did not become blinded by their successes. They introduced reforms in all aspects of life, from economic to political sectors. They improved their national capabilities in government leadership, endowments, industrial organization, social cohesion, and culture, attitudes, and values.

Singapore

Singapore, the smallest of these three countries, has three million people, limited territory, and virtually no natural resources. Unlike Hong Kong and Taiwan, Singapore is a multiracial country with a population comprising the three main ethnic groups in Asia: Chinese, Malays, and Indians. The country had a bitter experience with racial problems in the 1960s and, since the 1970s, it has striven for interracial harmony and cohesion. Its efforts have been largely successful.

Singapore has focused on improving its competitiveness in the economic sector. Its strategic location is only a small part of its competitive advantage. Important, too, is the fact that Singapore takes pains to reinforce the content, context, and infrastructure of its differentiation.

As an international hub, Singapore considers efficiency and transparency a necessity, while always remaining aware of the need to be responsive to constantly changing customer needs. The establishment of a relatively clean and competent government also commands respect. It has established clear regulations in the economic and business sectors. Singapore's goal is to have up-to-date technology, world-class infrastructure, open-minded people, and a well-educated workforce with world-class skills.

Singapore continues to press for improvements because of an ongoing sense of crisis. As a country without natural resources, it is attempting to make itself the most attractive hub in East Asia, whether as a major transportation terminal or a major financial and medical center. It is no surprise that Singapore has been largely untouched by the Asian crisis. Nor does it need to undertake drastic adjustments. Singapore is right on track.

Hong Kong
Hong Kong has had to cope with a wider range of challenges than Singapore. Under British rule, Hong Kong enjoyed competent and transparent government, an efficient legal system, wide-ranging political freedom, and a free press. However, since its return to China, it has had to exercise some prudence. Overall, Hong Kong is still in a relatively good condition. Like Singapore, it does not have to introduce radical adjustments in order to achieve economic recovery.

Taiwan
The most interesting case, however, is Taiwan. Under China's pretext of a One-China Policy, Taiwan is politically isolated by many countries as well as by the United Nations. Taiwan's location is not strategic. It has limited natural resources. In short, Taiwan is in an unfortunate position, but one that arouses a sense of crisis and survival.

Taiwan's position as part of the "Free World" during the Cold War helped to nurture this sense of survival.[18] The United States and Japan made Taiwan a low-cost manufacturing base for their old industries. Thanks to its sense of survival, Taiwan then developed its own industry and promoted its position as a low-cost manufacturing base for more advanced industries. Taiwanese products began to gain access into the international market. Initially, these products had the reputation of being mere imitations. But Taiwan continued to enhance its competence in production, technology, and marketing of manufactured products. Finally, Taiwanese products entered the world market respected for their quality and trademark.

Taiwan's capability of self-renewal has proven itself in other areas. In addition to being transparent and competent, the government is also visionary. It has striven to be successful in both the economic and political areas. By transforming itself into a democratic state with direct presidential elections, Taiwan's sustainability may be assured.

The success scored by the East Asian countries prior to the crisis prompted efforts to promote the welfare of all countries in the region. This welfare promotion was seen to lie in, among other things, higher workers' wages. This led to a new problem, because low wages had contributed to these nations' competitive edge. South Korea began to undergo an export decline in the late 1980s; it was followed by other East Asian countries in 1996. This was seen as a consequence of an increase in workers' wages rather than a drop in productivity. Most East Asian countries failed to immediately recognize the deeper problems affecting them. Some of them undertook creative destruction too late (see Box 2.3). So, the crisis set in.

Box 2.3

The Asian Sustainability Model: Three Failures

When a number of Asian leaders use certain elements of the "Asian values" concept to justify measures that may not reflect the needs, wants, and expectations of their people, this alone can lead to a negative

---

perception of Asian values. In fact, prioritizing economic development over political development, or the community's or family's interest over individual and public interest, or order over freedom, tends to inhibit dynamic economic development.

In the hands of a number of corrupt Asian leaders, certain Asian values have not only become a major constraint but have also reduced these leaders' ability to identify the signs of a looming crisis. Such was the case in South Korea, Indonesia, and Thailand — which suffered the most during the Asian crisis.

South Korea

South Korea is economically the most advanced of the three. Known before the onset of the crisis as the world's 11th-largest economy, South Korea had even become a member of OECD, a club of advanced countries, just a few months before the crisis set in.[19] Members of OECD are countries that are both economically and politically advanced according to their indicators of economic and political progress.

South Korea's GDP was one of the largest in the world, while in the political arena the country was known to be a model for implementing widespread democratic reforms.[20] This implementation of democracy included freedom of opinion (freedom of the press and the right to demonstrate), the freedom to set up political parties and organizations, including workers' unions, withdrawal of the military from the political arena, and direct presidential elections.

However, there was a difference between what was said on paper and what was done in practice. South Korea continued to maintain a closed market. South Korean companies continued to enjoy large-scale protection and facilities from the government, despite the fact that its products had been widely distributed in the global market.

It seemed an anomaly that the products of a country with a closed market could compete in the global market. A deeper analysis reveals that South Korean products generally sold to less-demanding customers who were more concerned with price than quality. When some South Korean products entered markets with more-demanding customers, these products rarely moved to the upper rank.

Nevertheless, South Korean companies grew into giant corporations. Yet, many of them were not competitive. The South Korean government intentionally tried to make South Korean companies grow into giant corporations dealing in wide-ranging business lines. The government made available low-interest bank loans without insisting on good feasibility studies. Also, these South Korean companies raised further funds through floating equities and debentures.

Surprisingly, few South Koreans voiced complaints against these practices. One of the reasons was the public's strong sense of nationalism. South Korean companies were bolstered in the hope that they could create high employment opportunities and at the same time fulfill all the needs of the South Korean people. This policy was implemented by prohibiting certain foreign products from entering the South Korean market.

Over time, more South Korean businesspeople traveled abroad and began to see that many foreign products were of a higher quality and value than South Korean products. They began clamoring for the import of certain foreign products, a situation that forced the South Korean market to open to these products. Soon foreign companies set up operations in South Korea.

As a result, competition became stiff. Signs appeared that South Korean companies were in fact non-competitive. Their non-competitiveness made it difficult to meet their sales targets. This resulted in their experiencing difficulty in servicing their debts, which had been extended in the first place without proper feasibility studies and proper debt-to-equity ratios. Things got worse because there was also corruption in the process of loan extension. A number of companies suffered ongoing difficulties in managing their debts, and many eventually could not repay them. A problem then arose because these bad debts were huge and involved a number of giant corporations, or *chaebols*, which were formerly expected to act as South Korean's economic engines.[21] The situation became aggravated when one of the *chaebols*, Hanbo, was pronounced bankrupt. This bankruptcy later prompted the South Korean government to undertake a massive investigation to find out the root cause of Hanbo's demise. The investigation revealed that some party leaders, and even one of the president's children, were involved.

Fortunately, the government could take firm action because South Korean democracy was already well implemented. Yet this action, though laudable, was too late. Bad debts were piling up, especially after the onset of the monetary crisis in Southeast Asia in mid-1997. The crisis had a considerable effect on South Korean companies, which had aggressively expanded their operations in this region as part of their efforts to establish Korea Inc.

Korea Inc., modeled upon Japan Inc., had a potential major problem because it was based on a strong desire to counter Japan Inc. in a short time. In an attempt to establish Korea Inc. quickly, the extension of bank loans ignored the prudential banking principle. Finally, South Korean banks found it more and more difficult to bear this burden, a factor that triggered the South Korean crisis. As a result, many South Korean companies went bankrupt.

This was tragic, because the crisis had its roots in a desire to bring about South Korea's glory in the world through its products and companies. Unfortunately, the process of translating this ambition into reality manipulated the "Asian values" notion, particularly with respect to placing the interests of the community over individual interests, which had even led to the emergence of blind chauvinism and rejection of openness. Although rejecting openness, South Korea nevertheless was able to transit from an authoritarian government into a democratic government. By not earnestly applying Western values, it missed the chance of finding out quickly whether South Korean products and companies were competitive.

Indonesia

Indonesia took a different road. It applied economic openness but did not follow it up with political openness. At first, this was something that indeed had to be done. Indonesia was then, and still is, Asia's third-largest country in terms of population, representing a huge market. Having an extensive territory and rich natural resources, Indonesia sustained political instability until the end of the 1960s.

Unfortunately, Indonesia's economic potential became meaningless in the face of prolonged political instability. Therefore, when the country began to rebuild its economic sector, it applied the Asian values in earnest, particularly with respect to placing order over freedom and prioritizing economic development over political development. All of this found expression in an authoritarian, undemocratic government under Soeharto.

Soeharto, with support from the World Bank, succeeded in kick-starting economic development, starting from food self-sufficiency and moving on to the transformation of Indonesia from an agrarian country into an industrialized one. The Indonesian government succeeded in reducing the number of poor people and promoting welfare. Indonesia became part of the Asian miracle and was even considered the next NIC.

This achievement made Indonesia nurture high confidence in its winning strategy. When the world needed an organization to speed up the process of globalization, Indonesia was not only active in the APEC forum but was also determined to speed up the process of trade liberalization. That was indeed a daring step considering that the institutionalization process had not run well as a result of the half-hearted implementation of democracy, and because Indonesian companies, many of which had been groomed through protection and their proximity to the center of power, were not yet competitive.[22] Trade liberalization obviously promised to make Indonesia more, rather than less, vulnerable. Because Soeharto adopted a number of measures recommended by the World Bank and the IMF, Indonesia was treated as a "good boy" by these two international agencies, which turned a blind eye to the potential problems that might arise in Indonesia when faced with trade globalization and liberalization.

When the crisis began, Soeharto initially tried to remain the "good boy" of the IMF and the World Bank by taking stern adjustment measures to deal with the crisis, even if he had to take firm action against his family members. The trouble was that Soeharto, who had half-heartedly implemented Western values, began to show inconsistency in putting Asian values into practice, favoring protecting his children and cronies from the stern adjustment introduced by the government to overcome the crisis. He even took measures that finally turned him into the "bad boy" of the IMF and the World Bank.

Soeharto paid a price for his half-hearted use of not only Western values but also of Asian values. Indonesia, previously predicted to be a country that could withstand the crisis, finally turned out to be the one worst hit by it.

Thailand

Thailand was a different case. Although triggering the crisis in Asia, Thailand was not as badly hit by the crisis as Indonesia. One of the reasons was that Thailand, which was the next NIC along with Indonesia, Malaysia, and the Philippines, did a better job of blending and applying Asian and Western values. This could be attributed to the unique character of Thailand. The country has never been subjected to colonialism and underwent little difficulty in establishing a nation-state. The only weak point is that it has been subjected to a great number of military coups. Yet, Thai political stability has not been much affected by these coups because its king is very much respected and loved by the entire nation. This was demonstrated when the country underwent a political jolt following a military takeover of power in 1992, which prompted resistence from Thai civilian groups.

As a guardian of Asian values, particularly with respect to placing order over freedom and prioritizing the interests of the community over personal interests, the King of Thailand canceled the coup and at the same time laid a foundation for establishing a democratic state based on a strong civil society. He also put an end to active military involvement in the political arena. Thailand had fully adopted the values of the West.

Nevertheless, Thailand had its own problems in applying both Western and Asian values. It began to lose steam in applying Asian values, such as frugality and industry, because of its high macroeconomic performance over a long period.

Unfortunately, something was forgotten in viewing Thailand's impressive macroeconomic performance: Thailand had yet to manufacture products that could compete in the global market. True, its agricultural products had successfully gained access into the global market. But because Thailand is not endowed with abundant natural resources, it needed to maintain a frugal attitude, but forgot to do so.

Both the Thai government and the Thai people were inconsistent in applying Asian values. Economic success over a long period of time and high optimism led many Thais to adopt a consumptive attitude. They began spending beyond their means. They borrowed from banks to purchase Mercedes automobiles and yachts. This was tantamount to depending heavily on their future income.

Unfortunately, when Thailand began to undergo a decline in exports, which was actually attributable to a drop in their competitiveness, the Thais did not view it as a danger signal. Even when they had become heavy borrowers of both domestic and foreign currencies, the Thais did not consider this a danger.

Only when their export activities continued to decline and many companies missed their sales targets, did they become aware of the looming danger. By then, Thailand had incurred huge loans in foreign exchange and many fell due for repayment. It was too late, however. Thailand then fell into the crisis, which later also dragged down other Asian countries.

How could this have happened? Most East Asian countries were blinded by their long record of high performance and by their Asian development model. In fact, the Asian development model had not escaped criticism, but little effort had been made to revise it because it was considered successful in bringing prosperity to Asia. Only after the crisis had set in and a number of Asian countries were badly hurt did these countries realize that the Asian development model required revision.

The Renewal Phase: From Bubble to Sustainable Asia

On July 2, 1999, *The Asian Wall Street Journal* introduced a new column titled "Asia's Changing Landscape."[23] The column stated that the question marks of whether the crisis was over were now gone, and that a new Asia, the result of a process of

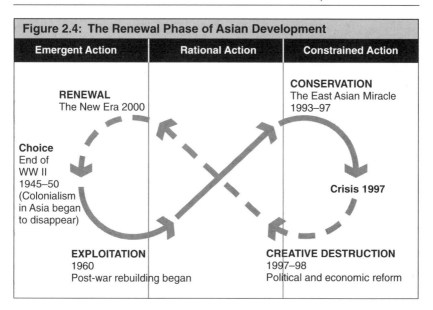

Figure 2.4: The Renewal Phase of Asian Development

renewal (see Figure 2.4), was emerging not only in terms of its economy and business practices, but also in terms of social and political reforms.

Thus, the Asian crisis, as well as causing a sharp drop in economic and political activity throughout the region, also served to bring its economic and political systems in line with the demands of the present day. This happened not only in those countries that were worst affected, but also in Japan, which escaped the crisis relatively unscathed.

This is a cause for celebration, especially because many economic, political, and social practices had for a long time been the target of criticism. The renewal process began in Thailand, not long after the country reached an agreement with the IMF to implement economic reform measures as a reward for its loan package. Thailand embarked on a vigorous campaign involving three government bodies and the international press to show that it was ready to reject its archaic practices.

This kind of determination is laudable. However, as David Hurst points out, the renewal process requires charismatic leadership.[24] The Thai prime minister, Chavalit Yongchaiyudh, did not fit this description. He was seen by many as indecisive and afraid to implement radical reforms. The country's determination to implement change, as shown by its campaign efforts, thus promised too much and delivered too little.

The Thai people were aware of the problem. A motion of no confidence was passed in Parliament, and Chavalit was overthrown and replaced by Chuan Leek Pai. But Chuan took the helm just as the crisis reached its peak. Indonesia and South Korea followed Thailand's example and turned to the IMF for assistance. Economic indicators did not immediately point to recovery despite Chuan's excellent qualifications to lead the process of renewal. He was clean, he was clever, and he was supported by a competent team of economic experts.

In time, however, Chuan's government took several successful steps toward political and economic reform. These steps attracted widespread support both inside and outside the country. The result was evident in Thailand's relinquishing of its position as the trigger for regional currency devaluation. A year after the onset of the crisis, Thailand was held up as a shining example of an economy on the mend, ready to achieve economic performance by implementing practices in tune with the age. Since then, the business landscape within the country's industrial sector has been enjoying profound changes for the better.

The next country to undergo a renewal process was South Korea. This ever-proud nation had just been accepted as a member of the OECD in 1997. When the country fell prey to the crisis, the South Koreans at first found it hard to accept the truth, but when they eventually did so, they faced it stoically. They took a number of steps to speed up the nation's economic recovery, indicating their willingness to sacrifice personal wealth in an effort to lighten the burden of economic reform, and to leave behind inappropriate practices.

South Korea should have had no difficulty in implementing the renewal process. In practice, however, it was another matter, especially after it was realized that these inappropriate business practices were the lifeblood of certain well-established groups, from unskilled workers to the business tycoons, or *chaebols*. A charismatic leader was clearly needed to implement changes and attract widespread support for them.

At first, this was difficult to achieve. The government of Kim Young Sam was rife with economic and political scandals, had been unable to keep South Korea out of the crisis, and simply could not be relied upon to lead the renewal process. In addition to obvious credibility problems, the government's mandate, obtained constitutionally, had come to an end.

Thus, the presidential election that took place in South Korea in December 1997 represented the country's intense efforts to create a platform for economic recovery and an arena for selecting a charismatic leader. One of the presidential candidates, Kim Dae Jung, had been a frequent contender for the post and was known for his reformist ideas. With his impressive track record, he was the obvious choice and was duly elected as the new president.

Although not yet officially inaugurated, in January 1998 Kim Dae Jung took a series of initiatives to kick-start the renewal process. These included holding open dialogues with the public that were broadcast on national television and covered all aspects of the economic situation and what should be done to rejuvenate it. The new president was also prepared to implement the bitter policies that were necessary for economic recovery.

This combination of approach and track record made it relatively easy for Kim Dae Jung to initiate the renewal process. Even the workers' movement, which really felt the effects of these harsh measures, gave the president their support, just as they had done in the old days when Kim was an activist struggling for workers' rights.

The *chaebols*, which had initially found it hard to adapt to the new conditions, had no choice but to acquiesce, especially when they saw that Kim Dae Jung did not have a conflict of interest with them. The *chaebols* slowly began to restructure their businesses and to introduce an element of corporate governance.

Since the South Korean people themselves were so committed to the renewal process, and because they had a charismatic leader, the country was able to turn its economic fortunes around in a relatively short time, and, backed up by more appropriate business practices, the country began to look forward, albeit tentatively, to the return of the Asian miracle.

Indonesia, the Asian country most adversely affected by the crisis, also made a direct attempt to implement the renewal process after it realized that it had no choice but to ask the IMF for assistance. Unfortunately, many groups were not prepared to go through with the reforms. This encouraged Soeharto, who was a charismatic leader, to adopt a half-hearted approach. There was also the president's ill health and concern about his continued ability to lead the government. In short, the people were not properly "conditioned" for the renewal process. This was in contrast to Thailand and South Korea, where conditioning had been an important factor.

It came as no great surprise, therefore, that Indonesia, which had entered the crisis in fundamentally better shape than either South Korea or Thailand, emerged as the least well-equipped to face it. Efforts to restore public trust by taking radical steps, such as those stipulated in a 50-point letter of intent did not count for much. Indeed, it is only recently that steps have been taken to implement the renewal process.

Preparations for reform should begin with the presence of a determined leader. Soeharto, who was seen to have failed to prevent the crisis from deepening, was clearly unqualified for the role. But as long as he remained strong politically, the Indonesian people had no choice. To make matters worse, Soeharto made little attempt to break with the old ways. This contributed greatly to the growing sense of public mistrust, and rendered ineffective any efforts to instigate the renewal process.

Soeharto was finally overthrown. This did not mean, however, that the renewal process would now progress smoothly. His successor, B.J. Habibie, had a credibility problem because of his long association with the former president. Although he took several successful initiatives that were in line with contemporary demands, he was less effective in leading the renewal process. Abdurahman Wahid, the new president, has succeeded in gaining international support, a step that is necessary to restore confidence in Indonesia's economy. However, Indonesia's problems are too complex to solve within a short period of time. Although Indonesia's economic indicators have shown positive signs of recovery, the process will take longer than it has in South Korea or Thailand.

In addition to these three countries, Japan has also begun to initiate the renewal process (see Box 2.4). This is proving to be difficult. Japan does not have a charismatic leader who is capable of both making the Japanese people aware of the need for renewal and leading the process. Thus, despite attempts to adopt modern business practices and corporate governance, there has been no major breakthrough of the kind witnessed in South Korea or Thailand. This prolonged the hardship, especially since Japan was expected to lead the recovery effort.

Box 2.4

Japan: No Longer Doomed?

By the first quarter of 2000, there was little doubt that something more positive was happening in the Japanese economy, despite fears that it might slip back into recession in the final months of 1999. Just as clear was that Japan's government was monumentally irrelevant to what was happening.

A new wave of enthusiasm was sweeping through a broad spectrum of the economy, including consumers, small- and mid-sized industries, large corporations, and an emerging, dynamic class of entrepreneurs, many of whom had previously been laid off or retrenched as a result of painful restructuring efforts. However, not all the news was positive. Bankruptcies had continued to climb, and unemployment was still just shy of three million, with young men especially hard hit.

Japan's hot and cold social and economic indicators said many things about Japan and its economy. First was that traditional enterprises that faced up to restructuring were beginning to feel the benefits, but that non-

---

traditional sectors were the primary — albeit emerging — engines of growth. Indeed, there were plenty of examples of traditional enterprises that restructured and focused on core businesses to lead their industries.

Shin-Etsu Chemical Company, for instance, had been shedding unprofitable operations and breaking profit records since 1995. Fuji Photo Film Company slashed corporate and divisional overhead and was sitting on a cash hoard of ¥380 billion. Companies in traditional sectors also benefited from the introduction of efficiency and productivity enhancing technology, powering up non-traditional sectors in the process.

The Japan Research Institute estimated in 1999 that large manufacturers and banks were investing ¥12 trillion a year in new enterprise systems. As a result of the Internet boom, personal-computer manufacturers were complaining that they could not meet the demand for cheaper, Internet-ready computers. Technology and Internet stocks drove 1999's 37% market surge, and 60% of Japan's Internet users said they had purchased products or services online.

Cellular providers and private courier services were also soaring. NTT DoCoMo — Japan's dominant cellular provider — grew into the fourth-largest capitalized company in the world after Microsoft, GE, and Cisco.

1999 also witnessed the high-profile emergence in Japan of four "net-batsu" — Internet conglomerates — that captured the imagination of consumers and politicians alike. After four decades of struggling against the odds set up by the old Japan Inc., a Japanese entrepreneur of Korean extraction — Masayoshi Son — was acknowledged to be rewriting the rules of Japanese enterprise.

At age 42, Mr. Son had built his Softbank conglomerate into a US$180 billion company with investments in 300 technology and Internet companies in the United States, Japan, Europe, and Asia. Close on the heels of Mr. Son was Yasumitsu Shigeta, a 35-year-old dynamo who had built Hikari Tsushin into a US$62.1 billion firm with revenues of US$2.4 billion. Hikari Tsushin boasted investments in 70 Internet and cellular companies in both Japan and the United States.

Trans Cosmos — run by 63-year-old Koko Okuda — was a somewhat distant third, with a US$11.3 billion cap. Masatoshi Kumagai, at age 36, had driven his company, InterQ, to a US$7.1 billion cap. About the role of non-traditional sectors in Japan's new economy, Mr. Kumagai said, "This is an opportunity that occurs only once in 100 years."[25]

Finally, traditional corporations were benefiting from the nascent Asian recovery, which boosted demand for Japanese products and made investment in offshore production capacity feasible much earlier than many expected. That bode well for the Japanese economy, too, because investment outflows by major corporations were expected to put downward pressure on the yen, increasing the attractiveness of exports.

The second thing we know is that Japan's recession and restructuring has produced a new breed of entrepreneurs aside from these non-traditional high-flyers. Growth of Japan's Jasdaq — a small-cap, over-the-counter market — is said to be largely attributable to new entrepreneurs. They are doing everything from rewriting the rules of competition in the entertainment industry, to providing outplacement services for cost-conscious enterprises. By mid-2000, Softbank's Mr. Son will have a high-tech bourse up and running — a joint undertaking with Nasdaq — which is expected to further catalyze high-tech entrepreneurship. As a result, it has frequently been suggested that established firms might soon be wringing their hands over attracting and retaining talented employees, rather than cutting the dead wood loose.

Third, we know that government was not just largely a bystander in Japan's off-and-on recovery — preoccupied with historic pump priming, which turned in only vastly disappointing results — but actually hindered recovery by impeding the pace of reform and restructuring. In the process, it produced a thunderously ominous debt bubble — equivalent to 114% of GDP — representing a huge obstacle to recovery.

Indeed, the government's reluctance to force restructuring of inefficient enterprises — and the banking sector — threatened to derail Japan's recovery.

First, the government was plowing even more public money into organizations that should have been allowed to die — to the tune of ¥25 trillion in 2000 — including murky credit associations, *shinkin* banks, and credit unions. The reason: to facilitate what the government terms the "smooth realignment" of the financial sector. And, despite increasing bankruptcies among small and mid-sizes firms that received controversial government-guaranteed loans, the government expected not just to extend the program, but to expand it.

Second, the government hadn't helped large firms to restructure by revising the notoriously outdated labor laws. As a result, most of the restructuring that had taken place was in smaller firms. In fact, almost 50% of employees laid off between 1997 and 1999 due to bankruptcy or restructuring were employed by small firms with fewer than 30 employees. Only 14% were employed by firms with 500 employees or more.

Large companies intent on rapid restructuring were still forced to pursue wildly inefficient — and unfair — strategies to slim down, such as reassigning unwanted employees to small subsidiaries and then liquidating them under a "special" scheme that placed a share of the burden of liquidation on creditors. Such liquidations were up by 120% in 1999.

When that didn't work, farmed-out employees were told that they had no chance of promotion or of an increase in salary, and there was little or no work to do. To add insult to injury, they were deprived of standard corporate perks, even e-mail addresses, increasing their sense of isolation. The intent was to deliberately humiliate the employees into retiring. So it was rich irony, indeed, that then Prime Minister Keizou Obuchi's avowed concern with employee welfare in fact translated into incredibly shabby treatment of employees, and that he believed his "kinder, gentler" approach to corporate restructuring was helping him politically.

Third, the government betrayed some truly bizarre notions of what economic recovery entailed. Mr. Obuchi said on January 1, 2000 about the government's new, uninspiring budget: "One can't kill two birds with one stone. Achieving economic recovery and fiscal reform at the same time is difficult. It is only after the Japanese economy regains stable growth that we can make plans to improve fiscal conditions."

The problem was that there could never be sustained recovery — despite corporate efforts to restructure and the growth of non-traditional sectors — without fiscal reform. It was clearly time for the government to get out of the way of reform so that the private sector might continue the business of rebuilding Japan.

Nevertheless, Japan's failure to position itself as "group leader" has also had its benefits. Asian nations now have the opportunity to formulate a model for economic development that is truly in tune with the demands of today's world, without having to rely on the vision and guidance of others. As a result, the East Asia of the future will develop far more dynamically, and will build on a foundation that is far more solid than before the crisis struck them down.

1 Dan Biers, "A Pause for Breath," in *The Asian Wall Street Journal's Asian Economic Survey 1996–1997*.

2 Ross Garnaut, "Overview of East Asia in Crisis," in Ross H. McLeod and Ross Garnaut (eds.), *East Asia in Crisis: From Being a Miracle to Needing One* (London: Routledge, 1998), pp. 22–26.

3 Ibid.

4 Noordin Sopiee, Director-General of the Kuala Lumpur-based Institute of Strategic and International Studies, is one of a small number of Asian intellectuals who view Paul Krugman's writing as an early warning, as seen from "Pump up productivity or fall by the wayside," in "Free Advice for Asia's Leaders," *The Asian Wall Street Journal's Asian Economic Survey 1996–1997*.

5 See the chronology of the Asian crisis compiled by Nouriel Roubini of Stern Business School, New York University, which can be obtained from http:/www.stern.nyu.edu/~nroubini/asia/asiachronologyl.html

6 An exception is Bank Negara, which began to tightly control loans to the property sector in March 1997, as disclosed in Nouriel Roubini's chronology of the Asian crisis, ibid.

7 Urban C. Lehner, "Does Corruption Stunt Growth?" *The Asian Wall Street Journal's Asian Economic Survey 1996–1997*.

8 In fact, the Russian crisis had, by then, claimed many victims. One of these was Long Term Capital Management, a fund management company whose customers were select people and whose core management personnel were the world's top financiers and two Nobel laureates for economics.

9 The crisis had also inflicted losses on a number of investment banking and other financial companies.

10 Dow Jones index, *The Asian Wall Street Journal*, March 30, 1999.

11 Philip Kotler, Somkid Jatusripitak, and Suvit Maesincee, *The Marketing of Nations: A Strategic Approach to Building National Wealth* (New York: The Free Press, 1997), p. 112.

12 Quoted from David Hurst, *Crisis & Renewal* (Boston: HBS Press, 1995), p. 71.

13 "Lure of the strongman," *Asiaweek*, June 13, 1997.

14 Su-Hoon Lee, "Crisis in Korea and the IMF Control," in Eun Mee Kim (ed.), *The Four Asian Tigers: Economic Development and the Global Political Economy* (San Diego: San Diego Academic Press, 1998), p. 211.

15 Ibid., p. 213.

16 For example, a *chaebol* in South Korea enjoys protection and interest subsidies in the domestic market.

17 Former Indonesian president Soeharto, Singapore's former prime minister Lee Kuan Yew, and Malaysia's prime minister Dr. Mahathir Mohammad are figures widely known to have put forward the concept of "Asian values" to defend their decisions to boost dynamic development in the economic sector while at the same time introducing restrictions in the political area.

18 Kwang Yeong Shin, "The Political Economy of Economic Growth," in Eun Mee Kim (ed.), *The Four Asian Tigers*, op. cit., p. 18.

19 Heather Smith, "Korea," in McLeod and Garnaut (eds.), *East Asia in Crisis*, op. cit., p. 66.

20 Linda Y.C. Lim, "Whose 'model' failed?: Implications of the Asian economic crisis," *Washington Quarterly*, Summer 1998.

21 Su-Hoon Lee, "Crisis in Korea and the IMF Control," op. cit., p. 213.

22 Hadi Soesastro, "Long Term Implications for Developing Countries," in McLeod and Garnaut (eds.), *East Asia in Crisis*, op. cit., p. 312.

23 See *The Asian Wall Street Journal* since July 2, 1999.

24 Hurst, *Crisis & Renewal* op. cit.

25 Kunii, Irene M., "Japan's net builders: Web entrepreneurs are out to win on a global scale — and bring profound change to Japan's business culture," *BusinessWeek*, March 6, 2000, pp. 18–22.

REPOSITIONING THE ASIAN ECONOMY

As Asia fell into crisis, many global investors who had previously been able to profit from its growth pulled out of Asia almost simultaneously and moved back to safer markets like America and Europe. But as the crisis began to show signs of easing and the economic indicators in several affected countries at last gave cause for guarded optimism, the Asian markets became attractive once more.[1]

At the same time, however, other regions competing for global investment also recorded good performance figures or favorable business conditions. The US economy, as evidenced by the Dow Jones index, was setting new records,[2] while Europe, with its newly introduced common currency, the Euro, looked increasingly attractive to the business community.[3] Eastern Europe and Latin America were showing signs of economic vitality and potential, and thereby attracting increased investor interest. Because these regions were ending the century on such a high note, people began to claim that the 21st century would be the Atlantic Century, not the Pacific Century.[4]

Under these circumstances, investors should have had no great need to invest in Asia. Moreover, institutional and company restructuring in a number of Asian countries was by no means complete.[5] Thus, investing in Asia was still a risky business, although the high-risk element made for possible higher returns than in either Europe or America. These two continents were "mature" and boasted relatively small populations of around 300 million inhabitants each. Meanwhile, Asia, besides being seen as a fast-growing area, had a population of 2.5 billion. This was a huge potential target market. Interestingly, since the diverse Asian currencies had been under severe pressure since the onset of the crisis, investing had become a cheap affair. Many American and European global players have consequently begun to overrun Asia, bearing investment portfolios and foreign direct investments (FDIs).[6]

This phenomenon, on the one hand, is a reason to celebrate. The restoration period is progressing well. However, the channeling of sizeable funds might give the wrong signals, especially when we realize that governments and institutions within the various countries are not progressing smoothly, nor are they able to implement solid marketing strategies.[7] The latest investments can only be used as a mark of approval from the international community for the steps and policies undertaken thus far.

In order to avoid a possible return of the crisis and to regain its competitiveness as the main target of global investment, Asia should break with the past by repositioning itself from "bubble" economy to "sustainable" economy. This repositioning effort must be manifested in a coherent strategy that is supported by appropriate tactics and values. Additionally, it should be substantiated by diligent reorganization of internal systems and institutional adjustments, which will be described in the next chapter.

The "bubble" condition of the Asian economy has been explained in Chapters 1 and 2. Thus, discussion in this chapter will focus on Asia's likely business landscape and strategy, which is based on the sustainable marketing enterprise model (explained in detail in Chapter 6). Although this model is generally used for companies, as shown later in Box 3.3, it can also be applied to a nation or even a region.

The Asian Outlook

Asia needs first to develop a strategic Asian outlook on its "business" landscape. This strategic outlook should attempt to analyze factors that influence Asia, either directly or indirectly. This will produce an environmental business profile of the main influences and a profile of the internal factors within the region. The strategic business outlook shows the position of the region and its level of competitiveness compared to other regions of the world. It addresses four factors: change, customer, competitor, and the company itself. Why these four factors?

In *The Mind of the Strategist*, Kenichi Ohmae explains that there are three players to consider in any strategy: company, customer, and competitor.[8] These three elements are known collectively as a "strategic triangle." Interestingly, although Ohmae also clearly explains the existence of a fourth "C"— *change* — he does not include it explicitly in his conceptual framework. This is perhaps because during the early 1980s when he wrote his book, business environmental changes were not as swift or complex as they are now.

Tom Peters, however, argues that business environmental changes must be incorporated in the formulation of any strategy.[9] Changes can happen quickly and unexpectedly, and can be complex in nature. Richard D'Aveni claims that changes are sudden and dynamic, which prevents building a sustainable competitive advantage.[10] Igor Ansoff claims that the level of turbulence within individual business environments is on the rise.[11] Thinking along these lines, then, the formulation of a strategic framework based on the sustainable marketing enterprise model must include a fourth "C" — *change*, as illustrated in Figure 3.1.

The first of these factors, *change*, specifically looks at the changes in technology, economic conditions, market dynamics, and political/legal and sociocultural conditions. The second factor, *competition*, comprises three dimensions: general, aggressiveness, and capability. The general dimension covers potential future competitors and competition from substitute products. Aggressiveness looks at the extent to which

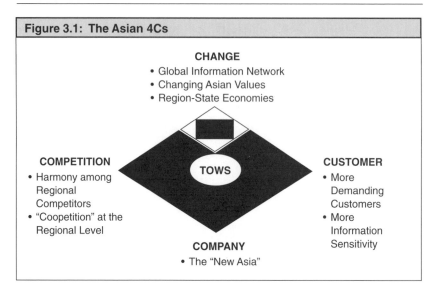

Figure 3.1: The Asian 4Cs

CHANGE
• Global Information Network
• Changing Asian Values
• Region-State Economies

COMPETITION
• Harmony among Regional Competitors
• "Coopetition" at the Regional Level

TOWS

CUSTOMER
• More Demanding Customers
• More Information Sensitivity

COMPANY
• The "New Asia"

competitors have implemented a creative and effective strategy. The final dimension, capability, deals with the competitive ability of competitors measured in terms of financial condition, people, and tangible (especially technology-related) assets. When assessing the third factor, *customer*, we will investigate the level of customer demand based on factors that have caused a shift in customer philosophy from "needs" to "wants" — and finally to "expectations." Finally, in examining the last factor, *company*, we will mainly take a look at the core-competencies issue.

We will now turn our attention to change, customer, competition, and company, in that order.

Change

Figure 3.2 shows several major forces of change that influence Asia.

Asia's technological mastery

The dynamic growth of East Asia over a period of 40 years had at its heart the development of technological skills.[12] Japan led Asia into the modern age, exporting outmoded technologies

80

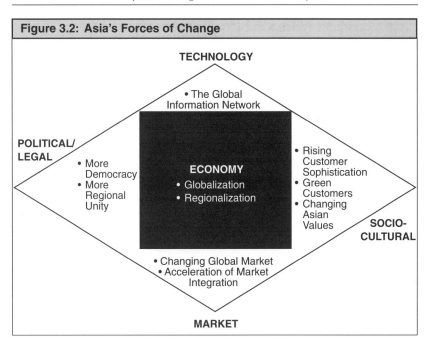

Figure 3.2: Asia's Forces of Change

and industries to other countries to the south along the lines of the "flying geese" model (see Chapter 1). These efforts not only encouraged the transformation from agriculture-based to industry-based economies in many East Asian countries, but also encouraged technological development and mastery.

By the mid-1980s, several Asian nations including South Korea, Taiwan, Hong Kong, and Singapore, had successfully made this transition, and had begun to approach Japan's level of technological mastery in everything, from automotive technology to semiconductors. They even started to follow Japan's example of relocating old technologies and industries elsewhere to countries such as Malaysia, Thailand, Indonesia, the Philippines, China, and India. These six nations themselves began to industrialize and develop their own technological skills. India even became an important global player in software technology.[13]

Of course, this dynamic growth was not limited to manufacturing technology, but also occurred in the field of transportation and telecommunications. East Asia became known for its rapidly developing information and communications technology. Several countries in Asia also began to look forward to the convergence of their infrastructure development programs, exemplified by the Singapore 21 and Malaysia's Multimedia Supercorridor.[14] Several countries cited the convergence of information technology and communications as a point of differentiation and the key competitive advantage in competing with other nations and global regions.

This convergence of technologies was used not only for interpersonnel communication — increasing the efficiency of management processes, marketing activities, and monitoring production processes — but also as a medium for new business activities, or "e-commerce." One look at the telephone density and personal computer (PC) penetration figures for Asia (see Figures 3.3 and 3.4) shows that e-commerce has not developed as rapidly in the region as in America and Europe owing to the low penetration rates of telephones and PCs.

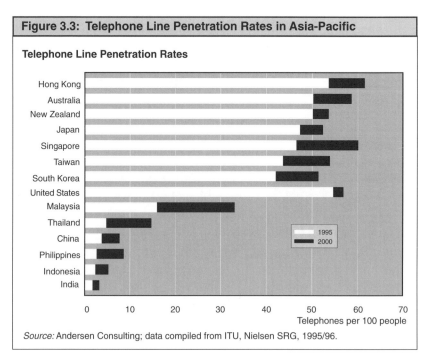

Figure 3.3: Telephone Line Penetration Rates in Asia-Pacific

Telephone Line Penetration Rates

Source: Andersen Consulting; data compiled from ITU, Nielsen SRG, 1995/96.

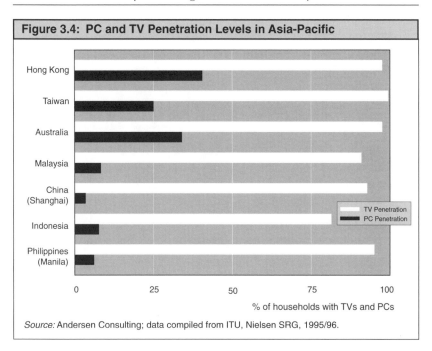

Figure 3.4: PC and TV Penetration Levels in Asia-Pacific

% of households with TVs and PCs

Source: Andersen Consulting; data compiled from ITU, Nielsen SRG, 1995/96.

Developments in information technology (IT) promise to improve Asia's performance and competitiveness (see Box 3.1). Speed and accuracy have become increasingly important, bearing in mind that many countries now compete with each other, thanks to these various technological developments. The risk is high for countries that are slow to implement such technologies, especially where their competitiveness is concerned.

Box 3.1

We Believe in him

"We believe in him," savvy Hong Kong investor and businesswoman Pamela Choy once said about Richard Li Tzar-ka, founder and chairman of Pacific Century CyberWorks, which in its first ten months grew an astounding US$33 billion in market cap. That would seem to say a lot about Mr. Li's management and entrepreneurial skills. But, perhaps surprisingly, those skills don't account for Ms. Choy's faith.

"Even if something happens to CyberWorks," Ms. Choy said, "it will be okay because of the father." Mr. Li's father is the legendary Li Ka-shing, who, if not Asia's biggest billionaire, is almost certainly its most respected, despite the inevitable detractors. And Ms. Choy's comments say a lot about residual mindsets in the New Asia.

Ms. Choy believes that Li Ka-shing's sense of honor and responsibility would never allow his son to fail. Meanwhile, his son, understandably and publicly, is consistently at considerable pains to demonstrate his independence from the senior Mr. Li. In fact, the elder Mr. Li — ever the opportunist — began investing in Internet plays after his son did.

Still, selling the younger Mr. Li's independence is tough. Richard Li's first high-tech venture — selling satellite-based communications systems to corporations — was sold to one of his father's companies when it tanked. But that bit of history demonstrates why Ms. Choy's faith may be well placed. There is a problem, though, and that is that CyberWorks has grown so big so fast that its capitalization rivals that of Li Ka-shing's flagship brick-and-mortar holding company, Hutchison Whampoa.

Indeed, in contrast to his initial techno dud — which followed the successful start-up and cash-out of Star Television — early developments at CyberWorks were phenomenal, as in the pleasantly ethereal — or Internet — sense. In January 2000, Richard Li announced that the company's investments had already generated a paper profit of US$1.3 billion. Of course, little of that was from actually selling anything.

Instead, it reflected the appreciating value of strategic investments which CyberWorks had made. About 20% of the US$1.3 billion profit that Mr. Li had announced — US$205.5 million — came from a single investment in Internet incubator CMGI. (A September 1999 share-swap valued at US$350 million grew to about US$910 million in a four-month period.) Twenty-eight other Internet- and technology-related investments provided the balance of the paper profit. On top of that profit, the value of CyberWorks' own shares increased by about 110% from mid-December 1999 to mid-February 2000.

As a result of the enthusiasm which investors were showing for the stock — despite technology and Internet sector volatility on the Nasdaq in early 2000 which also rocked Asian markets — as well as Richard Li's capacity to attract new investments, the spate of acquisitions, and the reported development of about 130 domains that will provide content for CyberWorks when it begins operations, Merrill Lynch in early February 2000 reiterated a buy recommendation for CyberWorks to investors, with a HK$25 12-month target. When the recommendation was made, CyberWorks was trading at below HK$18.

"As an investment vehicle, we think CyberWorks is an attractive means to play the development of the Internet in Asia,"[15] Matei Mihalca, Merrill Lynch's Asia-Pacific Internet analyst, said by way of explanation. Mr. Mihalca's enthusiasm, however, had less to do with CyberWorks' own product and service development, than it did with its investment in the other Internet start-ups, especially CMGI. In fact, he wanted Richard Li to open the spigots further.

"CyberWorks must begin to take larger stakes in earlier-stage opportunities," Mr. Mihalca said, and "with CyberWorks' new (financial) abilities, this should be possible." Richard Li in fact set aside US$200 million for CyberWorks' acquisition spree, and suggested the money would go a long way: "Most companies want to take our shares instead of cash." As a result, and despite the bevy of acquisitions made, only US$60 million in cash had actually been spent from the funds earmarked for investment in January 2000.

Richard Li had also earmarked close to US$600 million to do something no one else has, which was intended to be its principal business: developing content and television programming and arranging its delivery via satellite and cable. And doing it for the region. Not only has no one else managed to accomplish that feat, but those that have tried — Time Warner and Microsoft, for instance — have emerged badly scarred.

Nevertheless, enthusiasm for CyberWorks and other Asian Internet- and technology-related plays in 1999 and the first quarter of 2000 clearly rivaled that for Internet and technology pioneers listed on US bourses. CyberWorks' capitalization was bigger than Amazon.com's. But it also exceeded that of Cathay Pacific and Merrill Lynch, and approached that of GM.

So, it wasn't surprising that, as in the United States, ominous warnings about the perceived unrealistic values given to virtual corporations were on the rise in Asia in response to the region's own "Nasdaqian" frenzy.

Those concerns didn't put off investors, however. CyberWorks expanded its relationship with CMGI, forming a holding company for 18 of the US incubator's start-ups, and forged a separate link with Japan's second-largest Internet play, Hikari Tsushin. The tie-up — majority owned by Hikari Tsushin — also invests in Internet-commerce start-ups.

Sociocultural aspects

Increasing customer sophistication. The ever-accelerating free flow of information has enabled consumers to obtain information about the best and cheapest products available anywhere in the world. This transparency has caused a customer shift away from "enlightened" to "informationalized" attitudes. The word "consumer" here includes not only external and internal customers, but also investors. In the macronational context, these are the agents of a country's economic development. Consumers not only have rising expectations, but they are also now more "empowered" to realize their expectations. This shift from "enlightened" to "empowered" has given rise to a new breed of customer, one who is both highly critical and very demanding.

Global information has also encouraged a shift in consumer behavior from a traditional "needs-based" pattern, through a "wants-based" interim stage, toward a more "expectations-based" approach to buying. A failure to read these changes could have fatal consequences for a country.

Green customers. Although the number of industrialized countries in East Asia has increased, environmental issues have not yet become important, unlike in America and Europe. In Asia, it is common to find industries polluting the environment through particle emissions and wastewater. In addition, many industries upset the balance of nature by polluting their surroundings in the search for fossil fuels.

It is not only the immediate surroundings that are adversely affected by unscrupulous behavior, but the whole planet, through global warming. Consequently, many countries are moving toward the ratification and strict implementation of international trading standards covering the environment.

As people worldwide become increasingly concerned about environmental issues, companies are affected in three ways. They have to monitor environmental developments; they have to respond to these developments; and they have to work proactively to incorporate them in their business practices.

Unfortunately, too many countries and companies think of environmental investments as hurting their competitiveness. This perception is false, according to Michael Porter in his article "Green and Competitive: Ending the Stalemate," written with Claas van der Linde and published in the September–October 1995 issue of *Harvard Business Review*.[16] Porter and van der Linde suggested that competitive power springs from increasing the productive use of resources, and that this productivity never ends. All forms of pollution are manifestations of economic waste — for example, resources used inefficiently, or valuable raw material discarded. Improving environmental performance through better technology and methods, then, will often increase productivity and offset — or partially offset — the cost of improvements. This implies that environmental regulations should focus on reducing the transaction cost of the regulations themselves, which adds neither environmental nor economic value, but which facilitates product and process innovation. Corporations or countries should see environmental improvement not as a regulatory matter, but as an essential part of improving their productivity and competitiveness.[17]

Changes in Asian values. Asian values first received worldwide attention when East Asian countries began to record dynamic levels of growth. They were credited with being one of the causes of the region's success. Then, when Asia fell apart, they were widely held to be responsible for its downfall. The meaning of Asian values before and after the crisis, however, has remained the same.[18]

What, then, caused something that had previously been regarded as a recipe for success to suddenly be seen as a recipe for failure? The rapid development of IT and communications not only served to facilitate access to information, but also speeded up and heightened the intensity of cross-cultural and sociopolitical exchange, and the meeting of different values between countries.[19] This inevitably led to culture conflicts, which were concerned not so much with winning and losing as with the ability to achieve synergy.

Previously, therefore, Asian values could indeed be seen as a factor in Asia's success. Their tenets were conducive to the development of the "other" (that is, outside Japan) Asian economies — and even to the rise of Japan itself after World War II. At that time, the number of educated people was very low, as was the level of prosperity. Under such circumstances, governments tended to be regarded as omniscient bodies, able to steer a country along the best course.[20] At the time, governments were led by heroes who had freed their respective nations from colonialism or tyranny. They were, therefore, justified in placing order above freedom, and economic development above political development.

But the heroes of old should not remain today's heroes. The old heroes are counterproductive as the level of education and prosperity rises, and as access to information becomes easier to obtain.[21] Unfortunately, the confrontational response of several Asian leaders, especially the use of the "order over freedom" adage, constituted a cynical manipulation of Asian values. By contrast, the dynamic economic development sweeping across the region demanded swift and appropriate decisions on the part of individual governments.

Asian values are still relevant in today's societies, as they contain certain principles that are both positive and universal. However, Asian values do not contain all the necessary components required by the dynamic changes taking place today — most especially, the existence of a system that guarantees transparency and fairness.[22]

On the other hand, Western values may place too much emphasis on freedom and on the importance of the individual to be completely suitable for Asian cultures, which stress the importance of harmony. What we need is a hybrid: the best of East and West.

Political/legal aspects

The importance of democratic government. The increase in public prosperity and the changes in social culture among the Asian nations eventually began to influence political/legal aspects. East Asian countries previously controlled by an authoritarian government or military regime slowly began a transition to a civil and democratic government. South Korea, a country that had enjoyed economic success and which was established by an authoritarian military regime, began its cry for democracy after its people became prosperous and began to form strong civil movements in the early 1980s.[23] The struggle not only required great sacrifice, but also took a long time, only finally being realized in the early 1990s. A similar thing happened in Thailand,[24] the country with the most coup d'états in East Asia, which eased the military out of politics in 1992. Unfortunately, similar efforts by the people in the People's Republic of China culminated in the Tiananmen Square tragedy in 1989.[25]

The process of changing from authoritarian to civil governments was not only rocky, but also often stalled economic development. The best example of this is the Philippines. Following the People's Revolution, which ousted the authoritarian regime of Ferdinand Marcos in early 1986, the Philippines embarked on wholesale political reform. During this period, economic development became very much a second priority.

As Asians became more prosperous, they began to want a government that had a mandate to govern, was competent, and able to guarantee transparency and fairness. This is what happened when Soeharto, after 32 years in power in Indonesia, was forced to resign. He simply could not show that either he had a mandate, he was competent, or he could guarantee transparency and fairness.[26] Meanwhile, the Singapore government, which is often classed as "authoritarian," could demonstrate all of these characteristics, and the demands for democratic rule were muted.[27] Taiwan and Hong Kong, which held mandates, were competent and could guarantee transparency and fairness. They, nevertheless, needed to transform their governments, since they actually desired a population that is dynamic, both economically and politically.

Importance of regional unity. The need to create a dynamic economic and political community is not limited to one country, but also exists at a regional level. As a result of increased country interdependence within a region, regional groupings began to appear, such as the European Union (EU) in Europe, ASEAN in Southeast Asia, APEC in the Asia-Pacific, and the North American Free Trade Agreement (NAFTA) in North America. In the beginning, these organizations simply served as forums for economic cooperation.[28] However, the EU has since developed into a "supra-national" organization[29] that has the power to change national laws. The EU now has its own parliament and courts. Nevertheless, this model has not been emulated by other regional organizations.

Aside from supporting dynamic economic development within a region, a regional economic cooperative forum also acts as a facilitator in the global free trade movement through the ratification of trade liberalization agreements. This phenomenon is important, as it tends to reduce the role of an individual country in controlling its national economy.[30] Products are traded freely between countries, a process that is virtually unavoidable by any one individual government.[31]

These political-legal changes have not only lifted restrictions on trade, but have also given rise to the possibility of 100% foreign ownership of companies. Within Asia, there are several reasons why this has come about. Sometimes it is due to an awareness of the need to attract foreign capital to create jobs; at other times, companies are forced to acquiesce to foreign takeovers. This happened in Indonesia and Thailand during the crisis.[32] Foreign penetration has had a positive impact in terms of technology transfer. However, there have also been negative effects, as when some new foreign owners exploit local companies to serve their own interests. The impact of these takeovers should be carefully analyzed in order to minimize the damage to local companies.

Economic aspects

Effects of economic globalization. In the early 1960s, in the days before television became influential in daily life, Marshall MacLuhan wrote *The Global Village*, in which he claimed that the world was becoming one big global village. People could move easily from one place to another and have had speedy access to information about faraway events. Geographic borders and distances were diminishing.[33] On the human side, economic globalization was impacting the sociopolitical characteristics of countries as well as their economic arrangements.[34]

Economic globalization has been marked by the increased freedom of movement of goods and services between countries, the ability of companies to move into other markets, the dramatic reduction in the role of government in national economies, and the general trend toward market-based economies. Economic globalization has been driven by two swift, cutting-edge developments: first, the advances in information, communications, and transportation technologies with the rise of the Internet and terrestrial and satellite communications;[35] and second, the agreements on the liberalization of trade, products, and global investment.

The most significant impact of economic globalization has been increased free competition on a global scale. The freedom of companies to operate worldwide is regarded as a threat to local companies.[36] International companies generally enjoy levels of performance that greatly exceed those of their local counterparts. They have more advanced technology, more funds, and better-quality human resources and management capabilities. But there is a positive local benefit, too, in that this threat invariably encourages local companies to improve their performance. By forming strategic alliances, local companies can exploit these to gain knowledge and technology transfer.[37]

Economic regionalization as a vehicle for a new movement. Nation-states have begun to lose their influence.[38] They are no longer fully in control of their domestic market, nor can they distribute prosperity equally throughout the nation. Nations have been encouraged to exploit available markets around them,[39] both locally and internationally.

This has in turn encouraged countries in the same region to work together.[40] The next step has been the establishment of growth triangles, or what Kenichi Ohmae calls "region-states." Region-states are defined as an area (often cross-border) developed around a regional economic center with a population of a few million, up to 10–20 million, such as Hong Kong–Shenzhen, Taiwan–Fujian, and Singapore–Johor–Batam. These region-states have led to clearer and more rapid developments in regional cooperation in various spheres, which up until now had been merely agreements on paper,[41] including the promotion of harmony within region-states. One such region is the east coast of the People's Republic of China, which has experienced rapid growth owing to the establishment of ties with Hong Kong and Taiwan, which have vastly different political and economic systems.[42] The interesting thing is that the Chinese have even been willing to make dramatic adjustments to ensure that companies in Hong Kong and Taiwan can rely on China for support.

Market aspects

The global market change phenomenon. Intensive economic globalization means that local companies can no longer consider the domestic market as their own captive market. The global market has enabled players from all over the world to compete in domestic markets.[43]

The establishment of the global market has triggered global sourcing. Advances in information and transportation technology have enabled companies to source worldwide.[44] This includes almost all aspects within the value chain, from raw materials, through production, to marketing the finished product. Even though a country may lack the natural resources or fabrication facilities necessary for a particular product, it may still succeed in the industry if it has a wide enough network and a degree of technological mastery.[45]

Another development is that each country has had to deal with a shift from "product" market to "labor" market, and finally to "financial" market. Previously, economists worldwide viewed the market in narrow terms as a product market. As competition grew, each country felt the need to compete for quality employees in the global labor market.[46] Lastly, management also felt the need to attract investors in order to obtain strategic funds to support macroeconomic stability and further economic development.[47]

Accelerating market integration. Through several economic and regional cooperation forums, many countries are bringing their domestic markets in line with those of other countries. The problem is that, in many cases, the time frame for the implementation of agreements is generally too long.[48] The 4Is of investment, industry, information technology, and individual customers all need to be accommodated appropriately and reasonably quickly.[49]

Yet, sharp differences exist between the economies of nation-states or region-states,[50] resulting in difficulties in achieving harmony, not only with respect to trading and investment policies, but also within the legal systems related to transparency and fairness, financial institutions, infrastructure, and human resources. Lack of due care toward the changes needed in these four areas is one obstacle to the dynamic growth of a region.[51] This is what has occurred in Asia since mid-1997.

It is interesting to consider how the EU has integrated its markets. This has been done in two main stages. First, the markets of Western European countries that had no problems with harmonization were integrated.[52] Meanwhile, the countries of Central and Eastern Europe undertook efforts to improve their legal systems concerning transparency and fairness, financial institutions, infrastructure, and human resources. After a fixed period, they were considered to be not greatly different from those of Western Europe, and the integration of their markets was then effected.

In other words, market integration is concerned with sustainability. Efforts to speed up market integration should consider the ability of individual countries to unite harmoniously in all aspects related to business and the economy. If integration is effected too quickly, with large differences in economic resources prevailing between the countries or regions concerned, the result could be an increase in overheads rather than an increase in market potential. This is what happened during the first eight years of the German reunification, which caused the former West Germany a great deal of unplanned hardship.[53]

Customer

Who is the customer of a country or region?

The growing competition to attract global investors and a world-class labor force opens the question of who constitutes a nation's "customers." A government is no longer able to view its citizens or economic agents as its only customers, but also has to take into consideration global migrant workers and global investors. These are the people who will determine whether or not dynamic economic change occurs within a country. Even citizens of other countries should be included as a nation's "customers."[54]

It is, therefore, interesting to witness efforts undertaken by three Thai institutions not long after the country plunged into crisis and then requested assistance from the IMF. These institutions published an advertisement in several international newspapers that illustrated their understanding that the Thai government's "customers" were many, varied, and spread all over the world.[55] The advertisement began with an admission that Thailand had pursued policies that had thrown caution to the wind because it had become inebriated from the sustained period of success. It then announced their determination to adopt the radical adjustments required under the terms of the IMF package. It closed by saying that, after these adjustments were in place, Thailand would become attractive for all of its "customers."

Handling demanding customers

In line with regionalization, global workers, investors, and ordinary citizens from a particular country have become the customers not only of their respective nations, but of the region as well. Thus, attempts to attract these customers can no longer be undertaken by the country alone, but as part of a joint effort by all countries in the region. One example is the steps taken by the EU to introduce a single European currency — the Euro — only after first harmonizing trade, investment, and various legal aspects.[56] The varied efforts at harmonization have culminated in a more-mature Europe. Many customers within the EU now sense a new economic flexibility, and as a result the economy has begun to show signs of a dynamic recovery.[57]

On a more moderate level, many regional economic forums have also been set up with the aim of making their respective regions more attractive. These include ASEAN, which will implement AFTA in 2003. However, it must be admitted that policies such as these are more often related to achieving freer and faster movement of goods. Although this represents an interesting breakthrough, there are still problems with the implementation of payment systems to be used within a free trade area.

The difficulty lies in the fact that regional customers are not equally prosperous.[58] When one country runs into recession, customers will tar all countries with the same brush. This is what caused the crisis, which had begun in Thailand, to spread quickly to neighboring countries, as it was assumed that all countries in the region had the same problems. It mattered little to investors which countries had already implemented radical adjustments and which had not.

Under these conditions, countries that were in good shape actively approached customers to show that their countries' situations — macroeconomic and sociopolitical — were different, and that they had implemented radical adjustments. As an example, the new Thai government led by Chuan Leekpai invited global investors to Thailand and held a series of interviews that were covered in the international media. As part of Thailand's economic rejuvenation package, the country also implemented many other radical changes that have set it apart from its neighbors.[59]

Competition

When regional competitors strive for harmony

The changes triggered by technological, sociocultural, political/ legal, economic, and market factors, as well as customer definition, in turn caused changes in the competitive situation. Several changes led to intensified competition, not only at the regional level but at the global level too, in the form of inter-regional competition.

Many people have not yet comprehended the dynamic competition facing a country or region. A nation's competitive power is partly determined by its macroeconomic policies such as market openness and monetary policy. Beyond this, Michael Porter, in *The Competitive Advantage of Nations*, claims that the competitive power of a country or region is dependent on its ability to create an attractive business environment for companies. Porter claims that access to workers, funding, and natural resources does not fully determine prosperity, because a shortage of these things can easily be overcome. The prime determinant is industry and company productivity.

Thus, in terms of inter-regional competition, East Asia still needs to look at regional harmonization, whereas Europe has made great steps forward in this area, not only in terms of its trade and investment policies, but also in its supra-national legislation and government, and its single currency. For East Asia, such achievements will be hard to achieve, as there is no one country that is able or willing to take the lead. If harmonization is still needed, it must be conducted at the sub-regional level, through ASEAN, for example. This will also be effected to a limited extent through the implementation of trade and investment policies.

"Coopetition" at the regional level

If harmonization is difficult to achieve, then all the countries of a region should work together to create a regional climate that is conducive to investment activities and trade. Geographical location and sociocultural similarities, together with the existence of the overseas Chinese as a vehicle for change throughout Asia, are positive factors. The "ability to reform" is crucial for any country. Countries that are not capable of reforming, or are unwilling to reform, will impede the whole region's ability to attract global investors, global workers, and customers from other countries.

The countries of a region or sub-region must also compete among each other, and should not neglect to cooperate with other countries from different regions. This means they should engage in "coopetition" — namely, a combination of cooperation and competition.[60] Cooperation is created by establishing similar trade and investment policies, while competition derives from the development of reliable marketing strategies and strong financial institutions.

Company

Dynamic core competencies

After examining change, competitor, and customer, a country or region should try to assess its core competencies. Every country and region is like a "multi-business,"[61] with certain areas that are strong and others that are weak. Even the strong areas must be continuously upgraded. The competency of a country or region will mean little when competitors who have the same competencies but whose products are cheaper owing to their lower exchange rates or cheaper labor appear on the scene.[62]

In management, core competencies may be termed "dynamic" if they represent related skills in manufacturing products. If they relate to service, they will usually be of a more "permanent" nature. What is hard to emulate are core competencies supported by abundant natural resources and technological prowess. An example is the South African diamond business. South Africa possesses a wealth of diamonds and also has the technological skills needed for their exploitation. Thailand is another example, with its huge variety of fruit orchards and agricultural technological know-how. Unfortunately, not many countries are blessed with these capabilities. Usually, they have the resources or the technology, but not both.

In considering core competencies, a country or region needs to carry out a TOWS (threats-opportunities-weaknesses-strengths) analysis, a reverse of SWOT analysis. In this book, we prefer TOWS analysis because it starts with an outside-in perspective, whereas SWOT analysis uses an inside-out perspective. An inside-out perspective tends not to consider customers' wants or competitors' advantages.

The TOWS analysis is used because changes occur so rapidly that a particular advantage can be rendered meaningless in a very short space of time. Rapid changes often become threats to a company's survival, though they could also be viewed as opportunities. As an example, the Asian crisis that began in 1997 could cause the 21st century to be regarded not as the Pacific Century, but as the Atlantic Century. Weaknesses in spending power and economic activity may well cause Asia to lag behind Europe, which is now undergoing widespread harmonization. But Asia is a vast continent with a large number of countries and a huge potential market. Its infrastructures and systems, which form the basis of all business development, are not yet solid. There are also great differences in the speed of development within the region. But cultural approaches and the still powerful Asian values — including frugality, ambition, and hard work — may well compensate for these deficiencies and render them no longer an obstacle to Asia's ability to compete.

The Asian Strategic Architecture

Having analyzed the 4Cs, an organization must next forge an operational direction that will give it the ability to successfully compete and grow. As more businesses succeed in a country or region, so will the country or region succeed. The direction involves a complete system known as a "strategic architecture system." We will describe how this strategic business architecture works.

The Asian Strategy

The key to strategy is positioning. First, an organization must position on its organizational strengths. Second, its positioning should be unique to set itself apart from its competitors. Third, its positioning should be positive, believable, and relevant to the target consumers. Fourth, the positioning should be sustainable and not altered frequently until major changes in the business environment warrant a change. Positioning signifies the organization's "promise" to its target customers. Its positioning must be credible, and not earn a reputation for over-promising and under-delivering.

Based on these four criteria, the New Asia can position itself as "the world's largest diversified emerging sustainable economy." Asia constitutes the most densely populated region in the world, with more than 60% of the world's population. Asia also includes a great variety of nations, industries, and economic growth rates. Japan, for instance, a member of the G-7 group of nations, is highly developed, while Cambodia is only now starting out on the road to development. Asia's economic potential is unlimited. Clearly, Asia's size and potential could make it the world's fasting-growing region (see Box 3.2). This was plainly visible prior to the economic crisis. Even now, while most Asian institutions are still adjusting, many global investors are already back in town. They know that Asia offers the highest level of growth and that Asia's growth can be sustainable if it develops mechanisms and institutions that prevent a repetition of the recent crisis.

Box 3.2

Growing the New Asian Economy

By early 2000, it was clear that the Internet revolution had arrived in Asia. The same investor frenzy that drove US technology and Internet stocks to values that defied traditional attempts to determine their true worth was thought to have largely — alone — revised Hong Kong's economy. The South Korea, Singapore, and Taiwan markets grew strongly on the strength of technology and

Internet shares. Emerging markets likewise "leapt up from the deep abyss they fell into in 1997 and 1998 and trounced every developed world market, excepting only the mighty Nasdaq,"[63] growing 72% in 1999.

Although emerging Europe outpaced emerging Asia, information firm Morningstar's Asia index went up an impressive 69.4% for the year. And efforts by the US Federal Reserve chairman Alan Greenspan to slow the white-hot US economy by raising interest rates resulted in huge inflows into Asian stocks and mutual funds.

But there were better reasons than the dramatic run-up in Asian stock markets and mutual funds to believe that a new Asian economy was in the making. To be sure, the exhilarating advances in Asian technology and Internet stocks were as impressive as they have been speculative — and welcome. And in the long run, those bets were likely to pay off, for at least two reasons.

First, consider that throughout Asia's debilitating financial crisis, the technology, Internet, and infocommunications sectors continued not just to grow, but in many instances to grow dramatically in terms of revenue, headcount, and profitability. As a result, a good many Asian pundits began to point to these sectors as Asia's new engines of growth, as they have been for the United States for most of the 1990s.

Chances are, that won't be a bad call. But before we get to why, think about the reasons these sectors continued to grow over the two-year period during which Asia was agonizing through tortuous structural reforms and monumentally painful corporate restructuring. These non-traditional sectors were growing because a sizable segment of Asia's traditional enterprises — and individuals — were investing in their products and services.

Second, as Asia emerged from the crisis, that investment trend accelerated, reflecting the determination of Asian enterprise to become globally competitive and to capitalize on new sources of profitability.

Take technology. In 1999, PC sales hit an all-time high in Asia. Outside Japan, 14.1 million PCs were sold in Asia-Pacific according to International Data Corp., a 35.1% increase. South Korea grew fastest in terms of revenue, by a whopping 79.2%, or 15.5% of the market for the region. In China, PC purchases increased by 25.6%, to over 4.9 million, or 34.9% of the market. But Indonesia recorded an astounding 273.1% annual rate of growth.

IBM, the region's market leader in 1999, increased its Asian revenues by 39.7%. Chinese PC vendor Legend grew its revenues by 79%, providing a 7.1% share of the market, third behind IBM and Compaq.

Overall demand for servers in the region grew 21% in the third quarter of 1999, which helped to explain how Microsoft grew revenues for Windows NT and server applications by a whopping 82% in the same quarter. Even in Japan's still recession-plagued economy, Dell's sales grew by 30% over the first three quarters.

By 2003, there will be 80 million PCs in Asia, and 50 million of those will be Internet-ready. As for the Internet, China already has 10 million users, about a third of all users in the world. Revenues from Internet-commerce in China are expected to explode to US$3.8 billion in 2003 from US$8.1 million in 1998. By some estimates, Asia will capture 25% of global Internet-commerce revenues of US$1.4 trillion in 2003. In China alone, server growth is greater than 1,000% per annum. Dell already sells 40% of its PCs in Asia on the Internet, and 60% of Japanese users have purchased products or services online.

Then we have infocommunications, which includes everything from telecommunications to publishing to parcel delivery. Asia was expected to launch 73 new communications satellites between 1999 and 2008 in an effort to network the region and the global marketplace. "One Japanese official recently complained, no one wants to buy anything but computers and cellular phones."

Indeed, Japan's dominant mobile phone provider, NTT DoCoMo, one of the world's largest companies, was adding 18,000 new subscribers to its wireless Internet service daily in the first quarter of 2000.

Most Asian governments rightly recognized the potential of these non-traditional sectors early on. They developed plans for grandiose cyberports, technology palaces, and wired islands to embrace the New Economy while retaining a measure of control by managing partnerships between local businesses and multinationals.

The most recent of these is Hong Kong. Its chief executive, Tung Chee-hwa, under criticism for not doing enough to drive the economy into the wired future, in 1999 turned Richard Li — son of Hong Kong's fabled Li Ka-shing — loose to build a US$1.7 billion CyberPort designed to seduce technology multinationals and entrepreneurs alike to the former colony. And indeed, wild-eyed investors liked the idea enough to drive Cyber-Port's holding company — Pacific Century CyberWorks — to a market capitalization of US$33 billion in its first ten months in existence. Yet, it had only a trickle of actual revenue.

Malaysia's ornate Cyberjaya — *jaya* means palace — started taking shape before the crisis, but attracted only a fraction of the high-tech investment originally anticipated. Singapore's hugely hyped Singapore One — which wired the island with high bandwidth fiber optic cable — had signed up just one quarter — 25,000 — of the users it expected by end-1999. The island has over 700,000 dial-up users.

Thailand's much earlier effort to build a technology center by supporting local technology entrepreneur Charn Uswachoke — in a manner similar to Hong Kong's support of Richard Li — turned into an international public relations and business fiasco when the founder admitted to financial improprieties and resigned under pressure. His firm — Alphatec — made history in 1999 as the first company to be rehabilitated under Thailand's new bankruptcy law, but without the founder.

By now, it should be plain to the well-meaning leaders of these countries that state intervention is not what grows high-tech economies. Insanely creative, determined people do. And speaking of people, much of Asia doesn't have enough of the right kind of people — the engineers, software geeks, and visionaries that typify technology start-ups — to fulfill their high-tech visions.

Where large pools of the right people are available — China and Japan, for instance — their skills are generic, and require years of development. There is another problem, too. The source of "right people" — educational institutions — is insufficient in both the quantity and quality required to populate Silicon Valley wannabes. Every successful high-tech corridor in the United States grew up around highly respected educational institutions. And Asian governments serious about nurturing high-tech enterprise should have education as their priority.

Non-traditional sectors will be the engines of growth in the New Asia. But the evolution of high-tech Asian enterprise will take time, and it won't have much to do with fluffy government high-tech dreams. Non-traditional sectors grew during the crisis in response to the traditional sectors' urgent need to remake themselves, and consumers' determination to experience the benefits they offer. Not in response to government vision or intervention.

And it will stay that way.

The Asian Tactic

The main component of tactics is "differentiation." Differentiation has three dimensions: content (what to offer), context (how to offer it), and infrastructure (how to support the systems). There are three content components of New Asia's differentiation (see Figure 3.5). The first is: "The most populated and diverse economy." This differentiation is unique from other regions in the world. The second is: "The region-state economy." This emphasizes how the dynamic economic development in Asia — before the crisis hit — involved the formation of several region-state economies within Asia. The third is: "The corporate Asia." This emphasizes how dynamic Asian companies have surmounted geographical borders and political differences to serve the world market.

"Context" is the dimension that relates to how a company can deliver products and services to the customer. It comprises three parts. The first is "balancing." Dynamic and sustainable economic growth will be achieved only if there is a balance between the capacity to exploit the

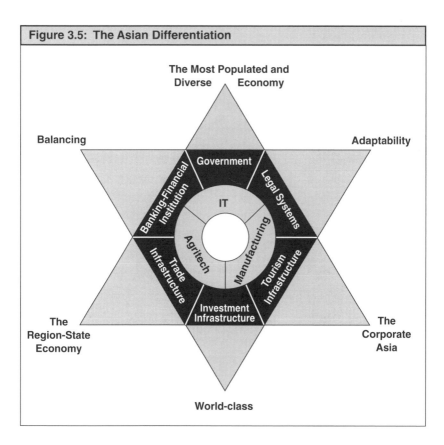

Figure 3.5: The Asian Differentiation

resources of a country or region and the needs of the customer. In Asia, with its varying stages of economic development, balancing can be maintained if the more advanced countries encourage their less-advanced neighbors to follow their lead. The second part is "world-class."[64] According to Rosabeth Moss Kanter, success in competing at the global level, whether between companies or countries, can only be achieved by those entities that have goods and services that fulfill world-class standards. Asia must have concepts, competencies, or connections so that it can act as either thinker, maker, or trader. The third part is "adaptability." Asia must be able to recognize changes in the business environment and adapt itself continuously to new challenges.

Infrastructure is the element that supports both content and context. It covers technology, facilities, and human resources. Technology includes information technology, and operational and factor endowment-related technology. For instance, Indonesia, with its fertile land, will develop agribusiness technology. The goal is to give each country or region unique competencies that will render it a superior competitor.

"Facilities" here emphasizes the need for widespread harmonization within a region of the banking and financial institutions and the governance and legal systems.

Human resources comprise the three elements that are vital for the effectiveness of any organization: leadership, managerial skills, and "followership." A country or company needs a leader who is not only credible but also a visionary, who can guide the process of change. Such a person will need managerial skills to organize the effort to fulfill the various wants, needs, and expectations of customers. Yet, this can only be accomplished if there is a high degree of followership from the organization's employees.

The Asian Value Proposition

Asia's products and services must deliver a value proposition that helps it to compete in the global market. Asia's value proposition should be "more-for-less" products and services. By buying Asian products, customers will receive more value for their money. This will be Asia's "brand."

Asia will be able to deliver "more-for-less" by adopting a process ("value enabler") that is geared toward achieving the highest degree of efficiency among competitors. In order to achieve a high level of efficiency, the New Asia employs three approaches: supply-chain management, market-based asset management, and innovative product development. The first of these is aimed at minimizing overhead costs that arise along the supply chain, and thereby creating an efficient business process. The second is aimed at optimizing market-based asset components — such as superior knowledge of business environmental conditions, or superior partnerships with suppliers and distributors. The third is aimed at achieving product and process innovations that lead to superior value offerings and efficiency.

Positioning, differentiation, and brand within the strategic business triangle of the New Asia, as shown in Figure 3.6, should be integrated and interrelated, and should act to strengthen the other two. If promises are to be credible, and a country or region is to be seen by customers as having integrity and a positive image, these promises must be supported by effective differentiation in terms of content, context, and infrastructure; positioning that is supported by strong differentiation that will in turn produce a strong brand and a positive image (see Box 3.3). If this is achieved, this strong brand will serve to strengthen its positioning. And if this process is allowed to continue, the result will be a snowball effect, as the three components become even stronger.

Figure 3.6: The Asian Strategic Architecture

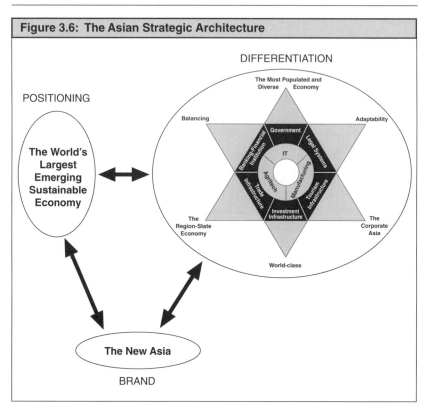

Box 3.3

Indonesia: A Nation in Transformation (Repositioning Indonesia in the Crisis Era)

Until the middle of 1997, Indonesia seemed like an economic miracle. The country had a huge market of more than 200 million people, sustainable growth, growth center areas spreading out throughout the country, improving lifestyle of its people, and social and political stability.

Such optimism suddenly turned into pessimism after a monetary crisis hit the country in July 1997. This crisis turned into an economic catastrophe, as reflected by the waves of corporate bankruptcies, employment lay-offs, and the liquidation of many banks.

The crisis worsened when the Indonesian government's efforts proved ineffective. The government invited the IMF to assist, but then often broke its agreements with the IMF. As a result, Indonesia's image suffered in the eyes of the IMF and the World Bank.

Political instability triggered by rioting in Jakarta, Medan, Surabaya, and Solo on May 13–14, 1998, and the controversial national leadership succession from Soeharto to B.J. Habibie on May 21, saw the crisis worsen. In response, foreign investors and even domestic business owners fled the country in fear of their lives. Their withdrawal paralyzed business activities in the country and caused a greater economic contraction.

The new government under president Habibie moved to stabilize and rebuild the country's image. Habibie worked hard to re-market Indonesia in order to attract foreign investors, but he was faced with the worst crisis in all of East Asia.

Repositioning Indonesia

Before the crisis, Indonesia had been very successful in attracting foreign investors and tourists. But after the May 13–14 bloodbath which claimed hundreds of lives, foreign tourists were averse to visiting the country. Likewise, investors were not inclined to invest their money in a country that had such high political risks.

Since the crisis, the Indonesian government has had to look for new ways to market the country. The old ways are no longer appropriate or effective. The country needs to reposition itself as the "New Indonesia" and promote "transformation" (see Box Figure 3.1). Indonesia must move toward ending an era of corruption, collusion, and nepotism, and toward becoming clean, transparent, and professional (see Box Figure 3.2).

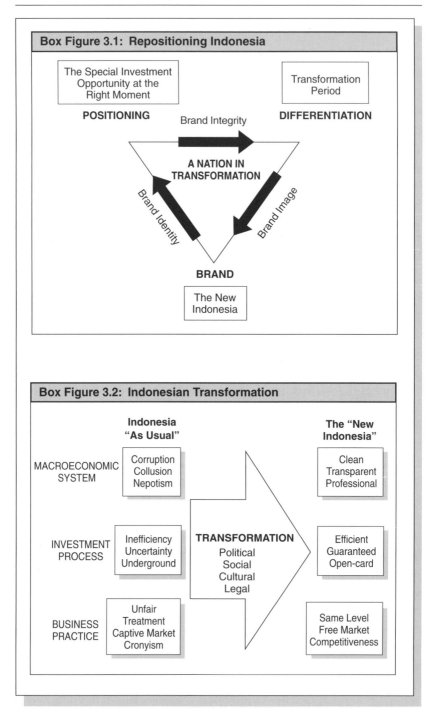

Box Figure 3.1: Repositioning Indonesia

The Special Investment Opportunity at the Right Moment

Transformation Period

POSITIONING

Brand Integrity

DIFFERENTIATION

A NATION IN TRANSFORMATION

Brand Identity

Brand Image

BRAND

The New Indonesia

Box Figure 3.2: Indonesian Transformation

Indonesia "As Usual"

The "New Indonesia"

MACROECONOMIC SYSTEM — Corruption Collusion Nepotism — Clean Transparent Professional

INVESTMENT PROCESS — Inefficiency Uncertainty Underground — **TRANSFORMATION** Political Social Cultural Legal — Efficient Guaranteed Open-card

BUSINESS PRACTICE — Unfair Treatment Captive Market Cronyism — Same Level Free Market Competitiveness

Indonesian government officials and business operators need to focus on providing timely and unique investment opportunities for would-be investors, especially those from Europe, the United States, and the Middle East. These opportunities should be backed with incentives such as tax holidays and effective bureaucratic procedures. At the same time, Indonesia should promote its differentiation, including its huge market, abundant natural resources, cultural and natural attractions, and the friendliness of the Indonesian people.

Tourist products should also be promoted to foreign tourists. Bali should be promoted to tourists from Australia and New Zealand, Manado to Japanese tourists, and Batam to Singaporeans.

Finally, the Indonesian government should provide investment and travel security for investors and tourists, to overcome concerns about personal safety.

Source: Trade, Tourism, and Investment Agency of the Indonesian Chamber of Commerce. Hemawan Kartajaya is Chairman of Indonesian Trade, Tourism, and Investment (TTI) Agency of the Indonesian Chamber of Commerce (1998–2002).

---

1   "Too good to be true," *Asiaweek*, April 30, 1999.
2   As of May 10, 1999, the Dow Jones index stood at 11,031.59.
3   See "Brave New Europe," *Fortune*, December 21, 1998; and "The Year of Europe," *The World in 1999* (The Economist Publications, 1998). In *The World in 1999*, Europe was even said to have a higher GDP growth than the United States and Asia.
4   In line with the introduction of the Euro and the mega-mergers between Europe and America, the 21st century has started to be referred to as "The Atlantic Century" (*Business Week*, February 8, 1999).
5   The process of creating an appropriate financial monitoring system is not yet functioning effectively in many countries affected by the crisis, including Japan, South Korea, Indonesia, and Thailand. The same is true of corporate governance.
6   In addition to entering the Asian regional stock markets, global investors have carried out FDIs by acquiring or purchasing shares in Asian countries affected by

the crisis. In 1998, FDI was sporadic; however, by 1999, a massive effort was underway. This happened even in Indonesia, which as of mid-May 1999 involved high political risks.

7   Jay Solomon, "Indonesia's sale of assets finds a momentum," *The Asian Wall Street Journal*, May 10, 1999.

8   See Kenichi Ohmae, *The Mind of Strategists* (New York: Penguin Books, 1982).

9   See Tom Peters, *Thriving on Chaos* (New York: Alfred A. Knopf, 1987).

10 See Richard D'Aveni, *Hyper-Competition: Managing the Dynamics of Strategic Maneuvering* (Toronto: The Free Press, 1994).

11 Igor Ansoff and E.J. McDonell, *Implanting Strategic Management* (New York: Prentice Hall, 1980).

12 This 40-year period begins with the rebuilding of Japan and the start of its period of growth, followed by the development of its Asian neighbors to the south.

13 The development of India's software industry is based in Bangalore.

14 A full picture of the initiatives of Asian countries in preparing their infrastructure can be found in "Asia's Information Infrastructure Initiatives," in *Electronic Commerce: Asia's New Emerging Market* (London: The Economist Intelligence Unit and Andersen Consulting, October 1996).

15 "Merrill: HK Pac Century CyberWorks 12-Mo Target of HK$25" (Dow Jones Newswires), January 27, 2000.

16 Michael E. Porter, *On Competition* (Boston: Harvard Business Review Books, 1998), p. 9.

17 Ibid.

18 Linda Y.C. Lim, "Whose 'model' failed?," *Washington Quarterly*, Summer 1998.

19 Kenichi Ohmae, *The End of the Nation State: The Rise of Regional Economies* (New York: The Free Press, 1995), p. 28.

20 Ibid., p. 11.

21 Ibid.

22 Lim, "Whose 'model' failed?," op. cit.

23 "Lure of the strongman," *Asiaweek,* June 13, 1997.

24 Lim, "Whose 'model' failed?," op. cit.

25 Michael P. Todaro, *Economic Development in the Third World* (London: Longman, 1997).

26 Hadi Soesastro, "Long Term Implications for Developing Countries," in Ross McLeod and Ross Garnaut (eds.), *East Asia in Crisis: From Being a Miracle to Needing One* (London: Routledge, 1998), p. 312.

27 "The Asian Economic Crisis: The Challenge for Government Policy and Business Practice", Asia Society publication at http://www.asiasociety.org, April 27, 1999.

28 Ohmae, *The End of the Nation State*, op. cit., p. 2.

29 Robert Cottrell, "Lots to be Doing in Europe," in *The World in 1999*, op. cit.

30 Ohmae, *The End of the Nation State*, op. cit., p. 11.

31 Ibid., p. 68.

32 The Indonesian Monetary Authority allows foreign banks to hold up to 100% of shares in a local bank. An example of this in practice is Standard Chartered Bank, which has majority share ownership of Bank Bali (*The Asian Wall Street Journal*, May 5, 1999).

33 Ohmae, *The End of the Nation State*, op. cit., pp. 2–5.

34 Ibid., p. 44.

35   Ibid., pp. 2–5.

36   Niraj Dawar and Tony Frost, "Competing with the giants: Survival strategies for local companies in emerging markets," *Harvard Business Review*, March–April 1999, p. 119.

37   C.K. Prahalad and Kenneth Lieberthal, "The end of corporate imperialism," *Harvard Business Review*, July–August 1998, p. 76.

38   Ibid.

39   Ohmae, *The End of the Nation State*, op. cit., p. 3.

40   Ibid., p. 82.

41   Ibid., p. 84.

42   Ibid., pp. 82–85.

43   Ibid., pp. 3–5.

44   Ibid.

45   Ibid., p. 11.

46   Ibid., p. 4.

47   Ibid., pp. 2–4.

48   An example is the proposal to bring forward the date for the formation of AFTA (as agreed by the ASEAN countries in 1997) from 2008 to 2003. This topic is described fully in "ASEAN: Regionalizing Asia," in *Competing in Asia: Forging Success from Complexity* (London: The Economist Intelligence Unit and Andersen Consulting, 1997), p. 10.

49   Cottrell, "Lots to be Doing in Europe," op. cit.

50   See *Competing in Asia*, op. cit., pp. 8–9.

51   Lim, "Whose 'model' failed?," op. cit.

52   Cottrell, "Lots to be Doing in Europe," op. cit.

53   Barbara Beck, "Germany's Chance to be Different," in *The World in 1999*, op. cit.

54   Ohmae, *The End of the Nation State*, op. cit., pp. 2–5.

55   See *Time, Newsweek, Fortune, Asiaweek,* and *Far Eastern Economic Review*, September–November 1997.

56   See "Europe's adventure begins" and "Europe's new currency," *The Economist*, January 2, 1999.

57   See "Will it be the Atlantic Century?," *Business Week*, February 1999.

58   Ross H. McLeod, "Overview of the East Asian Crisis," in McCleod and Garnaut (eds.), *East Asia in Crisis*, op. cit., p. 7.

59   See *Time, Newsweek, Asiaweek,* and *Far Eastern Economic Review*, February 1998.

60   This term occurs in Adam M. Brandenburger and Barry J. Nalebuff, *Co-opetition: A Revolutionary Mindset that Redefines Competition & Cooperation* (New York: Currency/Doubleday, 1997).

61   Ohmae, *The End of the Nation State*, op. cit., p. 65.

62   Ibid.

63   Tamzin Booth, "Emerging markets on the march again; Investors scour the globe for bargains," *The Wall Street Journal Interactive*, February 26, 2000, Internet edition.

64   Rosabeth Moss Kanter, *World Class* (New York: Simon & Schuster, 1995).

CHAPTER 4

RESHAPING ASIA'S CULTURE AND VISION

The Chinese term for crisis, *wei-ji*, has two components, danger/threat (*wei*) and opportunity (*ji* — actually, *ji hui*).[1] These two faces of crisis have become apparent in Asia since the events of mid-1997. The region-wide crisis resulted in a sharp decline in economic activity and buying power in various Asian countries, as well as increasing the number of poor people.[2] However, it has also provided the opportunity to replace various practices that have long been accepted as an unavoidable reality with practices more suited to the demands of economic growth.

As an example, Japan has begun to undertake radical adjustments, such as reducing the domination of industry by the *keiretsu*, removing the limitations on foreign ownership of shares of Japanese companies, and amending the lifetime employment practice. Such steps would have been unimaginable in the past.[3]

Of course, more radical adjustments had to be undertaken by countries that received IMF support, such as Thailand, South Korea, and Indonesia. These countries were forced not only to adopt austerity measures, but also to accelerate liberalization of their domestic markets. The latter was part of an effort to attract global investors and to accelerate economic restoration.[4] In addition, the crisis had encouraged more deliberate government policies and private business practices, owing to the improvement in market institutions, regulations, and competition.[5]

When Asia has recovered from the crisis as a result of making these various radical adjustments, its long-term economic prospects will be the best in the world[6] since the region possesses many natural resources and a huge population that is able to serve as both manpower and market. The region's current low income and consumption levels can only strengthen its growth prospects. Moreover, the favorable long-term economic fundamentals of flexible wages and prices, entrepreneurial populations, high savings rates, and, in the case of South Asia and Southeast Asia, favorable demographics (low dependency ratios for the next 30 years), will ensure that Asian countries, once they have recovered, will grow faster than the rest of the world for many decades. A number of economic policy reforms will likewise ensure a more efficient channeling of foreign funds into domestic investment and growth. Foreign investment will increase, due to the removal of barriers to entry and the lower prices in foreign currencies of regional assets.[7]

In short, the Asian crisis is not the end, so much as a new beginning. It may be a blessing in disguise. Because it took place before world trade liberalization had been fully implemented, Asian countries still have time to renew themselves and be ready when that time comes.

In conducting their renewal, Asian countries need also to renew their missions and visions, which would incorporate their objectives, aspirations, principles, and economic development values. Asian countries can then formulate these new missions and visions into simple sentences, as has been done by Singapore[8] (see Box 4.1). It would be useful to do this so that every economic actor in these countries may obtain guidelines as to the direction in which they should go. In addition, Asian countries should formulate a mission and vision statement for the Asia region, particularly since they will have to compete with other regions. As part of an Asian mission and vision, Asia should adopt a combination of Asian and Western values that can become its "regional culture."

Box 4.1

Singapore Vision 2000

The vision for Singapore is to become an advanced and globally competitive knowledge economy within the next decade, with manufacturing and service as its twin engines of growth.

It strives to be a knowledge economy where the basis for competitiveness will be the capabilities and intellectual capital to absorb, process, and apply knowledge. To achieve that, Singapore intends to have a strong technological capability and a vibrant entrepreneurial culture that thrives on creativity, nimbleness, and good business sense. To develop into a knowledge economy, Singapore should be an open cosmopolitan society, attractive to global talent, and connected with other global knowledge nodes. There should be a critical mass of Singaporeans who are risk-taking entrepreneurs, innovators, and arbitrageurs. Together with the global talent, they will move Singapore ahead in the Information Age.

Manufacturing should remain an integral component of the Singapore economy, with capabilities in the entire manufacturing value chain beyond production, from research and development (R&D) and design, to marketing and sales. At the same time, Singapore should develop into the premier service hub in Asia with a global orientation, with strong competencies in both its existing hub services as well as in new, high-growth services.

Singapore should strengthen its successful partnership with foreign multinational corporations, build up domestic capabilities, and forge strategic linkages with the region. Successful local enterprises should be nurtured into world-class companies. The workforce should be cost-competitive, motivated, and highly productive, with world-class capabilities in business management, technology, innovation, production and service, and international market development.

Source: Committee on Singapore's Competitiveness, Ministry of Trade and Industry, Republic of Singapore, November 1998.

On the other hand, to ensure the success of Asia's repositioning, Asian countries must "redesign" their organizations. This organization redesign should entail the creation of a unified image of Asian nations, which are currently divided into various sub-regional groups, by looking at the European Union as a model. This could be achieved by forming an "Asian Union," or even the "United States of Asia." This would not be an easy task, especially if one considers the experience of the European Union, which is relatively homogeneous yet required a long time to become the "United States of Europe." However, it must be admitted that the Asian crisis has encouraged several Asian leaders to understand the need for Asia's unification, at least monetarily (see Box 4.2).

Box 4.2

Is There a Case for an Asian Monetary Fund?

In September 1997, before the full international implications of the Asian crisis had become apparent, Japan proposed the establishment of a New Asian Monetary Fund (AMF). Far from undermining the role of the IMF, the AMF could act as a regional complement to the IMF in the way that, for example, the Asian Development Bank (ADB) complements the work of the World Bank. The sources of this complementary area are essentially fourfold:

- The Asian crisis has demonstrated the need for an early warning system. While the problems of one or two of the Asian countries were anticipated before July 1997, the extent of the meltdown and contagion took international institutions by surprise. Thus, ways to provide forewarning of impending problems are needed, and could be most effectively undertaken at the regional level, through the AMF, as the participating countries would have detailed knowledge of problems in their area.
- Once a problem has been identified, a country needs to address it speedily. Given the damage that contagion can produce, regional peer pressure through the AMF could be an effective method ensuring that this is done.
- Given its informational advantage and regional location, an AMF would likely be more responsive to a regional crisis than a global institution.
- The resources that the IMF initially made available were insufficient to head off the Asian crisis, and additional packages had to be hastily assembled as the crisis unfolded. The AMF could provide such a line of defense on a permanent basis.

The initial proposal for the AMF suggested funding of US$100 billion, half of which was to come from Japan and the remainder from China, Hong Kong, Singapore, and Taiwan. The argument was that such a sum would provide sufficient liquidity to forestall speculative attacks on the region's currencies. Unlike the IMF's loans, the AMF's assistance would not come with economic conditions attached.

Despite strong support from Malaysia, the proposal did not get far. Only two months after it had first been suggested, it was turned down at the fifth APEC meeting in Manila. One objection was the fear that financial support without any attached conditions would raise the risk of moral hazard. Another risk was lack of coordination and of potential conflict with the IMF.

Nevertheless, during the IMF/World Bank Annual Meeting in 1998, Japan returned with a more modest revised proposal, the Miyazawa Plan. This proposed a US$30 billion package for the region. Half of the money was to facilitate short-term trade financing; the other half was to promote economic recovery through medium- and long-term projects. Japan suggested that the Japan Export-Import Bank, the World Bank, and the ADB could all participate in the undertaking. In addition to the US$30 billion assistance plan, at the October 1998 APEC meeting, Japan and the United States, with the support of the ADB and the World Bank, launched the Asian Growth and Recovery initiative that envisaged a package of US$10 billion for the crisis-affected countries.

In the face of increasing instability of global financial markets, the need for regional institutions to dampen financial contagion is being increasingly acknowledged. Western Europe has a comprehensive regional financial infrastructure in the form of the Economic and Monetary Union. However, no such institution exists in Asia, in the Western Hemisphere, or in Eastern Europe. Along with similar institutions for the Western Hemisphere and Eastern Europe, the AMF could potentially play an important role as a complement to the IMF in providing funds to crisis-affected countries and developing an early warning system. The implementation of such regional institutions as the AMF as part of the newly emerging financial architecture will help both to enhance the efficiency of global financial markets and to minimize their systemic risk.

Source: Asian Development Outlook 1999, p. 44. Reproduced by permission of the Asian Development Bank.

It should also be noted that this initiative will not bear any value if companies in Asia, which are important players in Asia's repositioning, do not adopt good corporate governance. For this reason, this chapter will also discuss the importance of implementing corporate governance by companies in Asia.

The Possibility of an Asian Union or a United States of Asia

In the two decades before the crisis that started in 1997, East Asia, unlike South Asia and Central Asia, was the most dynamic growth region in the world. Yet the nations of East Asia did not form a solid association along the lines of the European Economic Community, the Association of South American countries, or the African Union. ASEAN, which now has ten member countries in the Southeast Asian region,[9] does not accommodate countries located in Northeast Asia, such as Japan, South and North Korea, China, Taiwan, and Hong Kong. APEC,[10] though its membership covers all countries in East Asia, is still too extensive, because its membership includes countries in the Pacific region, such as the United States, Australia, New Zealand, and Chile. Even Russia, whose coastline borders the Pacific Ocean, has joined APEC.

The effort to form East Asia into a union has been slight.[11] Malaysia's prime minister, Dr. Mahathir Mohammad, suggested in 1989 the formation of EACC, or the East Asia Cooperation Caucus. However, his proposal failed when Japan, under pressure from the United States, became unwilling to participate. Mahathir's proposal was finally shelved when the Australian prime minister, Bob Hawke, proposed an association covering the East Asia and Pacific regions, including the United States, which was welcomed by many countries and resulted in the formation of APEC.

Had Dr. Mahathir's proposal succeeded, countries in East Asia would have obtained an integrated market with very high potential, along with the opportunity to become more successful in attracting foreign investment. It could have led to the harmonization of commerce, law, and education, and to a single Asian currency. However, an association that excludes the United States may well be regarded as a challenge to the world's single superpower, since by including China it threatened to create a second superpower.

Besides the "problem" of the United States, there was also the absence of a country that could take on the role of leader (see Box 4.2). Japan, in spite of having a larger economy than all the other countries combined and the world's largest foreign exchange reserves (US$217 billion), and serving as the largest aid donor in the world, could not lead the formation of an Asian Union, since many Asian countries, including China, still carry traumatic memories of Japanese occupation. As for China, in spite of having the largest population and serving as a motor of dynamic development in Asia, it was not ready to become a leader because it lacked the democratic process needed to lead other Asian countries.

ASEAN partners, namely the United States, Canada, the European Union, Japan, South Korea, Australia, and New Zealand, did not constitute a regional cooperation organization. Besides ASEAN, there are, in fact, other regional cooperation organizations in Asia, namely the SAARC (South Asian Association of Regional Cooperation consisting of India, Pakistan, Sri Lanka, Bangladesh, Nepal, and Bhutan) and the GCC (Organization of Arab countries in the Persian Gulf). However, these two organizations do not undertake much cooperation with ASEAN.

On the other hand, although Japan, South (and North) Korea, China, Hong Kong, and Taiwan are geographically located close to each other, there is no cooperation forum among these countries. This is due, *inter alia*, to the influence of Japan's colonization of other countries in Northeast Asia more than 50 years ago. That experience is not easily forgotten or forgiven, particularly by South Korea and China. Thus, it is difficult for these countries to involve themselves in an organization with Japan. However, it is impossible to form a sub-regional organization in Asia without involving Japan. Ultimately, the

Northeast Asian countries appear to prefer not to form a regional cooperation forum.

Another factor preventing regional cooperation is the political status of some countries in the region. Taiwan, the official name of which is the Republic of China, is politically unrecognized in spite of its economic strength and despite having economic representatives in various countries acting as unofficial embassies. To China, Taiwan is no different from Hong Kong or Macao — namely, it is part of the PRC. It is difficult for China to participate in a regional cooperation forum that will put it on the same level with Taiwan or Hong Kong.

The interesting thing is that economic cooperation between China, Hong Kong, and Taiwan has been a fact since Deng Xiaoping became China's leader in 1979. By shaping an exclusive economic zone along China's east coast, Deng indirectly facilitated an active economic cooperation. Hong Kong and Taiwanese companies set up production in a number of regions along the coast. These companies were treated in the same way as those of other sovereign countries. Hong Kong and Taiwanese companies became deeply involved in the dynamic development of various regions in China.[12] The economies of the three countries seemed to become more and more integrated, and the area is now known as Greater China.

As a result, Northeast Asia was transformed into three main groups: Greater China, Japan, and the Korean peninsula (South and North Korea). The dynamic development of East Asia, post-crisis, will thus be colored by the "coopetition" between four sub-economies in the region — namely, Japan, the Korean peninsula, Greater China, and ASEAN. The four sub-economies together with SAARC will make Asia the biggest and most diverse economy in the world. This will depend on the ability of SAARC to increase the political stability in each member country as well as among countries in the region[13] because despite having a very large population, SAARC will need political stability if it is to achieve outstanding economic development.

The Importance of Regional Shared Values

Although a country or a region may use the tools of 4Cs analysis and TOWS examination, two other important things are needed:

- The country or region must own an inspiration or goal that goes beyond profit. It needs a vision (something to head for) and a mission (the way to realize the vision). Its vision and mission will inspire its resource allocation and guide its risk-taking.
- The region must form a strong culture that will guide the behavior of the government, the community, and business.

It must be admitted that it will be very difficult to achieve one regional culture. Asia is very diverse. There are the Indian, Moslem, and Confucian influences.[14] However, there are a number of similarities among the peoples of the region, such as thrift, hard work, and self-confidence. With globalization increasing the contact of the Asian community with the West, a number of other values are beginning to appear widely in Asia, such as respect for individual rights. Initially, this value was seen as "foreign" in a number of Asian countries. However, there is a growing realization that it is a universal value. This fits the global paradox that the more universal we become, the more tribal we act; the more we become the same in things economic, the more we become different in those things that represent our unique identities, including our language and our cultural history.[15]

Corporate Asia In The Future

Had there been no crisis, Samsung, Hyundai, Daewoo, LG, SK, and other *chaebol*s would have remained "The Untouchables."

124

But the crisis period halted their expansion and also led to outsiders, including foreigners, influencing these companies' operation.[16] The *chaebols* have had to divest businesses that are not essential to their continued survival.

They only illustrate the tip of the iceberg. In the Asian countries affected by the crisis, many company founders have had to loosen or renounce their control of their companies.[17] Needing money to settle their debts, they may have had to sell their companies at cheap prices.

Most Asian countries are not rich, and the crisis has made them poorer. Unfortunately, Japan, which normally would be able to help, was also facing hard times. Restoration was also difficult because many of these countries are too small to attract much foreign investment[18] and lack competitive strength. Some suffer from unstable political conditions. It is, therefore, likely that Asian companies and countries will increasingly turn to the West and reform their business practices according to Western standards.[19] This may lead in turn to the domination of Western companies in share ownership and company management. It could, ultimately, lead to a weakening of national sovereignty.

In the past, many Asian companies did not practice disclosure to their minority stockholders.[20] They felt that they were in a strong position. Investors, both locally and globally, fought for shares sold by management, of which there were relatively few. Now the reverse has happened. Investors are less interested in investing in Asian companies unless there is more disclosure. This is driving Asian companies into a new stage, that of being willing to embrace corporate governance. Asian companies are beginning to apply Western-style business practices, calculating the benefit not only to the shareholders, but also to the other stakeholders. Asian companies are finding that they must compete to gain the best customers, the best shareholders, and the best employees if they are to achieve sustainable prosperity (see Box 4.3).

Box 4.3

Hard Decisions in the New Asian Economy

Richina Media & Entertainment Limited — a venture capital firm specializing in media in collaboration with Ziff Davis, Times Mirror, and other international book publishing conglomerates such as Pearson Computer Books — experienced most of the varied and often bizarre growing pains that have become common anecdotal fare for companies struggling to attain a foothold in China and many other parts of Asia, according to its managing director, Agnes Ting. Richina's ventures mostly involve publishing technology-related magazines in China.

Ms. Ting — a publishing veteran who, before joining Richina, was deputy managing director of the *Far Eastern Economic Review* — says that her job was to bring a new level of professionalism to the organization, expand distribution, and introduce new titles to the marketplace. "I started by formally structuring the financial reporting line and human resources hierarchy. Every manager was given a specific set of responsibilities and authorities and targets of achievement," she told me recently.

That wasn't so easy in an organization that had been run prior to her appointment as many state-linked enterprises are — loosely.

"Of course, there were many people against these policies since, in the past, they had such flexibility and no real reporting line. There were many obstacles thrown up and much resistance from the staff. I had to coach, discuss, and talk with them one by one, set samples to show how things were to be done, and at the end, replace those who were adamantly against change or refused to cooperate.

"But gradually, there have been some that found the value of my policies," Ms. Ting says with characteristic humility.

In fact, she believes that developing a professional culture for the organization was her biggest challenge — and most important accomplishment. "Although the company has expanded quickly, the HR (human resource) and business systems were quite a mess when I came in. There were too many personal relationship kind of networks — or in other words, cronies were everywhere.

"I took six to eight months to replace and clean out the major ones (senior-level executives) by recruiting or by switching their jobs. Also, regular meetings are held so that we could carry on a two-way dialogue and ensure that messages were not distorted.

"The first few hires were done very carefully. First, I had to be sure they would be able to perform; and second, I needed to know they were committed, and had the persistence to stick with the job although the organization was still not free of the effects that personal relationship networks have on morale. Ultimately, the regular meetings and new recruits collectively proved to demonstrate the value of the changes I was advocating.

"As a result, over time more staff began to understand that all our plans were for the betterment of the company and for their self-development as well — and not simply a power show.

"I have to say that I was able to do these things because I have a very supportive board that understood the real situation and agreed that it was more important to clean and rebuild the foundation of the organization than to force further expansion on the not-too-solid foundation that existed then," she explained. For Ms. Ting to get the results the board expected, she had to approach her mandate in the long-term: with a solid organization, revenues and profits would follow.

And indeed, getting organizational culture and reporting relationships straightened out — or well on the way to being where Ms. Ting expect them to be — allowed her to turn her attention to growing the company.

Although the effects of the Asian financial crisis had left the China market significantly less scarred than most of the rest of Asia, it did complicate her work.

That was at least in part because Ms. Ting intended to distinguish her titles from the competition by investing in quality. "Since local publishing is still not very sophisticated, other than presenting readers with high-quality editorial, Richina introduced improved production technique and design," she explained. "We provided light-weight coated paper, full-color printing, and gate fold, centerfold foldouts to focus attention on the quality of our advertisers' image and reputation."

That's a work still in progress. "We aim now to upgrade our facilities — which include a full pre-press center — to international standards," as a result of the initially warm acceptance in the marketplace and the need to stay ahead of the competition.

The company is positioned to make those investments, however, in large part as a result of two important developments during Ms. Ting's tenure. First, the company broke even last year, and expects to be profitable this year. Second, Richina recently sold its interest in a separate joint venture with Ziff Davis to the international publisher.

The sale follows a successful four-year partnership that saw its titles achieve the success necessary to support Ziff Davis's own management infrastructure. Because that investment is now justified as a result of the market development work undertaken with Richina, Ziff Davis is expected to expand rapidly over the next several years.

But for Richina, the success of the venture translates into additional resources that can be ploughed into strengthening its own business. Indeed, after human resource — and a quality product, of course — Ms. Ting believes that capital is crucial to rapid growth and the capacity to dominate the industry segments at which her titles are directed.

Ms. Ting's accomplishments are testimony to a new reality. And that is that in the New Asia, things are different, even in a marketplace infamous for doing business on the basis of connections and relationships within organizations and networks of organizations. The competition is learning from Ms. Ting that doing the right things at the right time are far more important.

And those that don't think so, will be eating Ms. Ting's dust.

Companies in Asia should recognize that they must deliver value to the customers, the employees, and the shareholders. Performance indicators to evaluate the company's ability to deliver value to the three main stakeholders include two dimensions: value levers and value risks. Value levers are those that can be controlled and managed by the company, such as customer satisfaction, return on investment, employee satisfaction, and so on. Value risks are those that cannot be controlled by the company, such as customer turnover, market sentiment indicator, employee turnover, and so on.

Beyond Good Governance

Lee Kuan Yew of Singapore had an authoritarian style of leadership, but unlike other Asian leaders, his leadership style was aimed at maintaining law and order, and at making the community and nation his number one priority. He also implemented proper strategic market planning to set appropriate industries in motion for Singapore. Thus, it is not surprising that Singapore was not badly impacted by the crisis. However, Singapore will face big challenges in the future and must avoid settling into complacency.

Simply carrying out good governance is no longer sufficient. To reach success, the government has to be a "real marketer" so that it can attract the best companies, the best global investors, and the best talents in the world to create a strong competitive advantage.[21]

1 Dan Waters, *21st Century Management: Keeping Ahead of the Japanese and Chinese* (Singapore: Prentice Hall Asia, 1991), p. 3.

2 See, for example, "Asia's meltdown," *Fortune*, February 16, 1998; and "Asia's puzzle," *The Asian Wall Street Journal*, October 26, 1998.

3 For examples, see "The right model for Asia", *The Asian Wall Street Journal*, October 26, 1998.

4 *Asiaweek* and *Far Eastern Economic Review*.

5 Linda Y.C. Lim, "The challenges for government policy and business practice," *The Asia Society*, April 27, 1999, p. 17.

6 Ibid, p. 17.

7 Ibid, pp. 17–18.

8 Report of Committee on Singapore's Competitiveness, Ministry of Trade and Industry, Republic of Singapore, November 1998.

9 Ibid.

10 Officially, APEC was established in 1993, through a meeting in Seattle, in the United States, of economic leaders of a number of countries in the Asia-Pacific region.

11 The "flying geese" phenomenon is an international work distribution phenomenon apparent in all the East Asian countries.

12 Jim Rohwer, *Asia's Rising* (New York: Touchstone, 1995), pp. 134–6.

13 Ibid., p. 192.

14 John Naisbitt, *Megatrends in Asia: The Eight Asian Megatrends that are Changing the World* (London: Nicholas Brealey Publishing Limited, 1995), p. 107.

15 Ibid.

16 Michael Schuman, "Korea's recovery suggests reform isn't the only key," *The Asian Wall Street Journal*, May 17, 1999.

17 Michael Backman, *Asian Eclipse: Exposing the Dark Side of Business in Asia* (Singapore: John Wiley & Sons (Asia) Pte Ltd, 1999), p. 100.

18 Lim, "The challenges for government policy and business practice," op. cit.

19 Ibid.

20 See also Backman, *Asian Eclipse*, op. cit.

21 Bruce Einhorn, Pete Engerdio, and Manjeet Kripalani, "Rebuilding Asia," *Newsweek*, November 29, 1999, pp. 68–75.

Revitalizing the Companies

ONLY THE SUSTAINABLE SUCCEED

5

When the Asian crisis hit, several major shocks were immediately felt by companies across Asia.[1] Capital flows to the region, which had continued to increase prior to the crisis, immediately reversed as investors' confidence in the region plummeted (see Figure 5.1). Sharp devaluation of Asian currencies caused increasing debt defaults for foreign debt and accounts receivables. Ballooning inflation and unemployment lowered consumer confidence and spending. Labor unrest was heightened due to lower wage increases, lay-offs, inflation, and ongoing uncertainty. The impact of the crisis on companies operating in the region was large and far-reaching.

Both the timing and magnitude of the crisis were unexpected. Many companies were caught off-guard. For some, the crisis simply worsened conditions that were evident prior to the crisis. Some faced ballooning debt burdens that forced them into bankruptcy. Some were acquired by companies with stronger financial capacity, mostly foreign firms. Not all companies, however, were hit hard by the Asian crisis; some even benefited, such as Jollibee Foods Corporation, the franchise-holder and operator of the Philippines' top fast-food chain.

Jollibee was ready for the recession in the Philippines. It had no dollar-denominated debt, it sold an affordable product, and it had a proven record of defending its turf against global

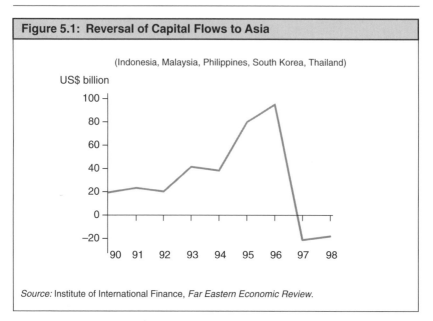

Figure 5.1: Reversal of Capital Flows to Asia

(Indonesia, Malaysia, Philippines, South Korea, Thailand)

Source: Institute of International Finance, *Far Eastern Economic Review.*

fast-food franchisers like McDonald's. Jollibee frequently ranks first in brand-name recall in local Philippines' marketing surveys. With the slump, Philippine consumers were cutting back on upscale dining, which helped Jollibee to post further gains. In the first half of 1998 alone, Jollibee reported a 33% rise in net profit on sales of 6.7 billion pesos.[2]

Companies in Asia responded to the growing crisis in different ways. A survey conducted by Andersen Consulting at the onset of the Asian crisis (in 1997) shows that most companies in Asia adopted defensive postures,[3] namely cost-cutting, postponements of new investments, portfolio restructuring, and debt restructuring (see Figure 5.2). Although defensive responses were necessary for short-term survival efforts, Andersen Consulting urged Asian companies to think longer-term by creating a breakaway advantage that would enable them to emerge from the crisis as winners (see Box 5.1).

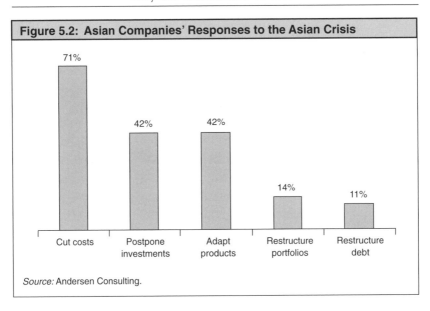

Figure 5.2: Asian Companies' Responses to the Asian Crisis

Source: Andersen Consulting.

Box 5.1

Creating the Breakaway Advantage: A Guide for Companies in Asia in Times of Crisis

After conducting a study of its clients in Asia, Andersen Consulting came up with a framework to help Asian companies conceive and capture "breakaway" advantage in the Asian crisis (see Box Figure 5.1).

The framework, called the "change axis," is composed of two dimensions of change: the magnitude of change, and the corporate focus of the change. The magnitude dimension indicates the amount of change that is taking place, which runs from adaptive (evolutionary changes) to innovative (revolutionary changes). The focus dimension, on the other hand, indicates the location of top management's attention in making the change, which runs from total organization (internal) to total environment (external) focus. Aligning the two axes,

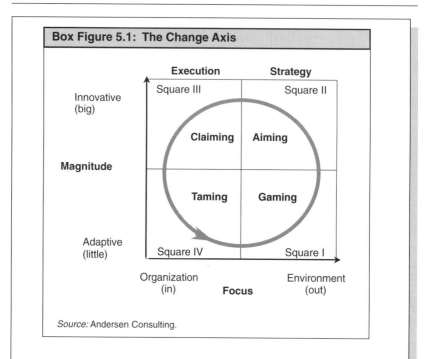

Box Figure 5.1: The Change Axis

Source: Andersen Consulting.

the "change axis" is divided into "squares" that describe the actions that organizations should be taking at any given time.

The four "squares" are: gaming, aiming, claiming, and taming. A company needs to change as it moves through these four stages. The goal of the first square, *gaming*, is to gain as much information and insight about the external world as possible. In gaming, Asian companies should use divergent thinking techniques — such as war gaming — in order to find new perspectives, innovate, and create options. Gaming is also a time for trial and error, and quick experimentation. There are no sacred cows in gaming; anything goes! Andersen Consulting believes that gaming is critical. Companies that do not game will end up with conventional perspectives and "me-too" strategies.

Square two, *aiming*, is where visions are set, goals agreed to, and strategies created in relation to the opportunities emerging in the external environment. Companies should evaluate options discovered in gaming, make decisions about goals and future directions, and envision unconventional ways to accomplish and achieve their mission. Most importantly, they need to end up with a plan of action.

Square three, *claiming*, is where the vision and strategies are operationalized through people, processes, and technology. This is where companies "stake a claim" by implementing the strategy for which they are aiming. To do this, companies must put the processes, technologies, and people foundations in place. Since claiming entails big organizational change, companies have to anticipate problems and mistakes. They need to create coherent actions among all people that are necessary to make it happen, establish open and consistent communication, and manage potential conflicts.

In square four, *taming*, profits are claimed and sustained through continuous improvement and operational efficiency. This is the period where calm and predictability return to the organization. Square four is where companies spend most of their time, because of the high comfort levels and attractive cost structures. However, companies should not be so engrossed in organizational issues that they miss the future. In addition, they should not allow managerial focus to become completely internal. And most important of all, companies have to avoid complacency. Instead, they need to start gaming again and go through the "change axis" continuously.

The "change axis" can be used to understand and guide the behavior of companies in Asia today. Catalytic events, such as the Asian financial crisis, move companies out of their comfort zone. However, in Asia today, many companies are limiting their strategic options: they are playing a cautious "same game" and ignoring the possibility of creating a new game altogether. Andersen Consulting's survey shows that most companies are responding to the crisis by retreating deeply into square four, which includes cost-cutting and downsizing, operational improvements, debt-restructuring, crisis management teams, and portfolio rationalization. For some companies, these actions are a necessary intermediate step for survival. However, both those companies that are in absolute paralysis and those that are relatively healthy must move quickly to spend time in square one in order to challenge conventional wisdom and capture their "breakaway" advantage.

Source: Andersen Consulting, "Creating the Breakaway Advantage," April 1998.

Aligning Competitiveness and Financial Soundness

To determine the appropriate responses for Asian companies, we devised a matrix that represents a "snapshot" of Asian companies' conditions at the onset of the Asian crisis. Using market competitiveness and financial soundness as variables, Asian companies may fall into one of the four cells: bubble, aggressive, conservative, and sustainable (see Figure 5.3). The best is, of course, the "sustainable" companies, those that have high global competitiveness and high financial soundness. To survive or emerge from the crisis as winners, Asian companies that fall into the other three categories (bubble, aggressive, and conservative) must eventually become a "sustainable" company by improving their competitiveness and/or fixing their financial problems.

To gain a clearer view of how the matrix can guide strategic thinking, let's look at how companies within each cell can improve their positions.

138

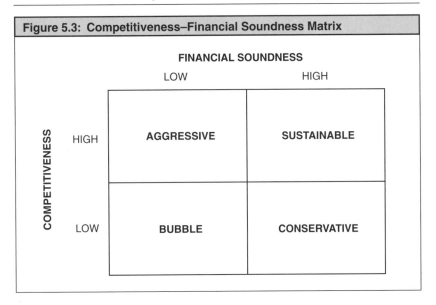

Figure 5.3: Competitiveness–Financial Soundness Matrix

Bubble Companies

There are many Asian bubble companies. Prior to the crisis, these companies generally lacked focus as they expanded their businesses blindly, often into sectors where they did not have expertise or strong competitive assets. Their competitiveness is low, since the companies' resources and focus are spread thin across many businesses. These companies are also typically highly reliant on massive debt-financing to fuel their expansion. When Asian currencies sharply devaluated, many of these companies fell into financial crisis as their debt burdens soared.

The Korean *chaebols* and many other Asian conglomerates are classic examples of bubble companies. The *chaebols*, which dominate South Korea's economy, have been so obsessed with growth that they built enormous overcapacity in major industries and piled up huge debt. Aggressive diversification into various businesses also corroded the *chaebol's* competitiveness.[4] They did not have the capacity to manage all of their businesses well, nor was the domestic market large enough to support them. The *chaebol's* business units are also too small to compete globally, since only a few of them can reap the economies of scale that global competitors enjoy or achieve the huge sales volumes necessary to maintain world-class research and development.

Companies falling within this category face the biggest challenge to emerge from the crisis as winners, or even merely to survive, since they must do a "vectoral shift" to become a sustainable company. The "vectoral shift" consists of two elements: improving the company's market competitiveness (the "vertical shift"), and improving the financial condition and management (the "horizontal shift") (see Figure 5.4). As with any vectoral movements, there are two ways to achieve a destination. The company can first do the "horizontal shift" (improving its financial condition by restructuring its debt and improving its risk management) before it does the "vertical shift" (improving its competitiveness by refocusing its business and reassessing its business strategy). Alternatively, the company can focus on improving its competitiveness first before fixing its financial problems. There is no best approach as to which shift to do first, since it depends on the particular challenges facing the company.

The best and fastest way, of course, is to adopt a comprehensive turnaround program that encompasses both competitiveness and financial improvements. However, only companies with strong management and financial resources can consider doing this. Most importantly, bubble companies need to start making some kind of shift (either horizontal or vertical), since failure to make any shift will drive the company into unprofitability or bankruptcy.

South Korea's Samsung Electronics is an example of a bubble company that is focusing on improving its financial condition first, prior to improving its competitiveness. As an initial step to restructure its business, Samsung Electronics has cut 27% of its workforce (16,000 people), discontinued 52 product lines, sold non-core assets such as an office complex in New Jersey, in the United States, and repaid US$4.7 billion in debt.[5] In addition, the company has cut many unnecessary

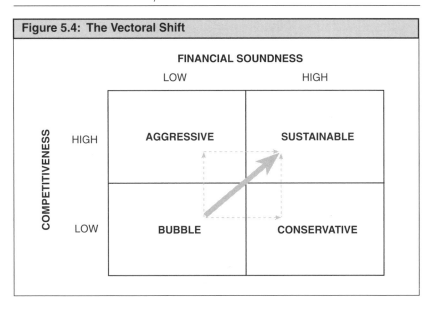

Figure 5.4: The Vectoral Shift

FINANCIAL SOUNDNESS

expense items, such as golf-club memberships, executive meals, and chauffeured company cars. The cost-cutting efforts are expected to save the company US$1.3 billion a year.

CEO Yun Jong Yong acknowledges that "restructuring is only the first step, since cost reductions will no longer produce big profits." He further elaborates that earnings will now come from intangible assets such as marketing abilities, brand image, and new product lines. Thus, while its cost-cutting efforts continue, Samsung Electronics is constructing a strategy to strengthen the company's competitiveness. A key plank of the new strategy is to focus on innovation and improve its research and development.

As another example, Daewoo, South Korea's second *chaebol* after Hyundai, intended to undergo both "shifts" at once. After growing into a sprawling global conglomerate in 32 years, Daewoo was forced to embark on a massive downsizing effort so as to shed its debt burdens and get the group into a lean fighting shape.[6] The group's pre-crisis aggressive expansion left Daewoo with US$50 billion of debt following the crisis, nearly five times the group's assets. Under pressure from creditors and the South Korean government, founder and CEO Kim Woo

Choong decided to sell all or part of Daewoo's most profitable businesses, from shipbuilding to luxury hotels, in order to halve corporate debt by the end of 1999. After the restructuring, Daewoo will concentrate mainly on making cars, plus trading and finance.

Consequently, Daewoo had about 30 divestment deals in progress that could bring in over US$6 billion. It landed a preliminary agreement to sell its auto-suspension manufacturing unit to Delphi Automotive Systems for US$113 million. General Motors may buy out Daewoo's share of several other auto-component joint ventures. Japan's Mitsui Engineering & Shipbuilding is eyeing Daewoo's profitable shipyard business, and European firms are looking into buying its truck and bus operations.

From these examples, it can be inferred that survival is the top priority for companies that expanded too fast. These companies must solve their financial problems by managing their short-term cash flow and containing risks that might jeopardize their survival. They must also refocus on core businesses that have a chance of becoming globally competitive, while selling, spinning off, or shutting down other businesses where they cannot achieve a competitive advantage. Whatever they do first, these companies cannot maintain the status quo, since doing so might bring them to the brink of bankruptcy.

Asian conglomerates' commitments to restructure, however, have proven "easier said than done." The South Korean *chaebols*, for example, have been reluctant to merge the operations of similar businesses.[7] They do not seem ready to take this step, despite the government's strong urging that they do so. While some have announced mergers of their operations (for example, Hyundai and LG will merge their memory chip operations), many have not taken the necessary steps to cut excess capacity through plant closures.

Aggressive Companies

Aggressive companies are those that enjoy strong global competitiveness but faced financial problems at the onset of the

Asian financial crisis, due to aggressive debt financing or imprudent financial management. These companies usually have strong competitive assets in the markets in which they operate, such as strong brands, effective marketing strategies, and economies of scale. However, due to overly high confidence, they rely on massive short-term borrowing (usually unhedged) to finance "good" projects or operations. As a consequence, when the Asian financial crisis struck (currency devaluation and high interest rates), they faced financial turmoil.

To improve their position, these companies need to make a "horizontal" shift to fix their financial problems, while maintaining their competitiveness (see Figure 5.5). They must still leverage their competitive assets by maintaining or improving their brand equity, product quality, and productivity (see Box 5.2). These challenges, however, are relatively easier to confront, since these companies' competitiveness is a good selling point when negotiating with their creditors or potential investors. Furthermore, these companies are usually run by a good management team.

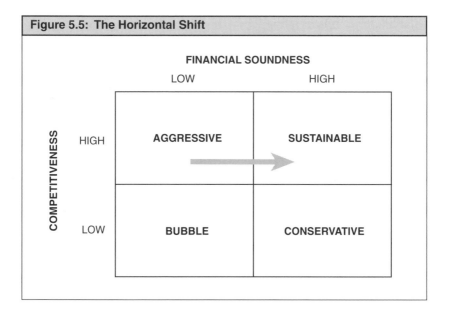

Figure 5.5: The Horizontal Shift

A good example of an "aggressive" company is Indonesia's Indofood Sukses Makmur (ISM), the country's leading processed food manufacturer.[8] Despite its young age (no more than two decades), the company has a portfolio of strong brands including instant noodles, cooking oil, food condiments, beverages, ice cream, and snack foods. Like other successful consumer goods companies, ISM has a strong distribution network in its main market, Indonesia, covering more than 100,000 outlets throughout the country. In its main business of instant noodles, ISM has a dominant position, holding 90% market share in the large Indonesian market. It has also defended its local market from global/regional players such as Maggi of Nestlé and President of President Enterprise. Furthermore, with an exponential growth rate in sales in the past eight years, ISM is now the largest instant-noodle producer in the world. ISM is one of the most admired companies in Indonesia and is capable of consistently delivering value to its main stakeholders: customers, shareholders, and employees.

Box 5.2

Siam Cement: Eating the Competition

As a giant Thai producer of cement, petrochemicals, pulp and paper, and steel, Siam Cement is not only strengthening its finances, as other Thai conglomerates are doing, but is also restructuring its operations and reorganizing its sprawling set of businesses into more streamlined units. These could soon buy out distressed competitors in the heavily glutted industries of cement and petrochemicals. "To be able to participate in distressed-asset sales, we had to consolidate our core business," said president Chumpol Nalamlieng. Selling off its ancillary businesses, and thereby reducing its debt, is giving Siam Cement the wherewithal to go on an acquisition binge.

Owned partly by Thailand's royal family, Siam Cement is the country's pre-eminent industrial powerhouse, with a highly skilled workforce of 30,000. Unlike most of its rivals in the Thai cement and petrochemical industries, Siam Cement adroitly shifted to an export-led strategy when the local economy nose-dived in 1997 — a testimony to the quality of its products. Siam Cement's pulp and paper division, for example, increased the export component of its sales from less than 10% in 1997 to nearly 50% in 1998. Such nimble strategic moves will keep creditors for Siam Cement's US$4 billion in debt at bay and allow the company to eke out a net profit of US$220 million for fiscal 1998.

The debt remains Siam Cement's most serious problem. Like other Thai companies, it found willing creditors and used cheap money to expand beyond economic reason. But unlike the products of many other Thai companies, Siam Cement's products are good enough to export and thus generate the dollar revenues it needs to keep its creditors satisfied. Siam Cement's stock, which was trading at US$11.50, has lost roughly two-thirds of its value over the past two years, a relatively resilient performance compared with many Thai stocks. But shares could jump as the company reorganizes.

Source: "The 1999 investor's guide," *Fortune*, December 21, 1998.

When the rupiah was devaluated, however, ISM's debt loads became very high, especially when only US$30 million of its US$1.1 billion debt was hedged. Yet, mainly due to the financial prowess of CEO Eva Riyanti Hutapea, ISM was able to resolve its problems by gradually hedging its debt. The latest data show that ISM has successfully hedged US$800 million of its debt. In 1997, it made the smart decision to "dump" all of its foreign exchange losses within one year. By doing so, it effectively avoided further cash flow loss to pay taxes. In 1998, ISM was back to profitability and its sales have continued to rise dramatically.

In addition to fixing its financial problem, ISM managed to improve its competitiveness. As the Asian crisis worsened, ISM found opportunities to leverage its economies of scale as the world's largest instant noodle producer and its low cost structure by making itself a regional company. ISM plans to do this by weaving a strategic alliance with First Pacific Limited of Hong Kong. First Pacific, which is 53.5% owned by the Salim Group, ISM's parent company, has been widely recognized for its capability in marketing and investment management in Asia. All said, ISM's sales and profits continue to grow despite the crisis still lingering in Indonesia.

Another aggressive company is Philippines' San Miguel. In its attempt to return to a healthy cash position, the food and beverage giant sold assets and wiped away debt.[9] They raised around US$1.2 billion in cash by selling off San Miguel's stakes in an offshore Coca-Cola bottler and a Nestlé subsidiary in the Philippines. With that cash, San Miguel paid off a huge chunk of the company's debt. For the first time in more than a decade, San Miguel has net cash on hand — about US$350 million, according to Merrill Lynch Securities in Manila — which it can use to expand capacity in its core beer and food franchises in the Philippines.

To maintain its competitiveness, San Miguel is planning to pull back from its investments in Vietnam and China and to focus on selling food and drink in the Philippines' market, where it has significant advantages, including its distribution network across the archipelago of 7,100 islands. Although many economists forecast a stagnant Philippines' economy for the near future, Filipinos still have to eat and drink. And in times of stress, consumers are even more likely to gravitate to familiar brands like San Miguel. The company is well aware of its strong San Miguel brand name, which is why the company has balked at self-destructive price cuts that might erode the value of its brand equity.

Conservative Companies

Conservative companies are those that have done relatively well financially during the Asian crisis, despite their lack of strong market competitiveness. There are two types. The first consists of companies that experienced windfall profits as a result of the crisis. Many Asian exporters that sell commodities fall within this category. Because of the devaluation of Asian currencies, these companies can offer very competitive (and even cheap) prices to the world market. As a result, they generally experience significant growth in revenues as they earn US dollars.

The second type consists of companies that were relatively conservative financially prior to the crisis. Thus, even though they are weak regarding competitive assets, they have been able to weather the crisis relatively well. Many Asian state-owned companies belong to this category (see Box 5.3). On average, they do not have much debt, since most of their projects are funded by the government.

Box 5.3

PLDT: Revitalizing a state-owned Telecom Company

"I almost died for this deal," Manuel V. Pangilinan, the charismatic and sometimes controversial president of PLDT, says about the hard-won acquisition of the Philippines' largest telecom and former monopoly. Mr. Pangilinan also heads up Metro Pacific and both companies' Hong Kong parent, First Pacific Group. In 1998, at the height of the Asian crisis, First Pacific paid US$749 million in return for control of 27.4% of the company, a 31% premium.

To acquire PLDT, First Pacific had to shed profitable assets to acquire the cash required for the purchase, and in the process became a much more focused conglomerate than it had pre-crisis, and set an example for other creaky groups, including its own larger parent, Indonesia's Salim

---

Group. "The move impressed plenty of bankers and investors, who saw Mr. Pangilinan making the hard choices to deal with the Asian crisis that many other regional executives still refuse to make,"[10] *The Wall Street Journal* enthused at the time.

The labyrinthine negotiations required to close the deal — restrictions on foreign ownership due to its strategic importance to the Philippines had to be skillfully navigated, and the holdout of a major shareholder almost scuttled arrangements at the last moment — clearly took a toll on the normally energetic Mr. Pangilinan. But when he says that he almost died for the deal, he's serious.

On the way by helicopter to a meeting south of Manila to discuss the terms of the acquisition, an engine failure caused Mr. Pangilinan's ride to crash into a line of trees, narrowly avoiding a power line, and slide down a ravine. No one was injured, but the near-death experience was symbolic of just how much First Pacific was betting on the outcome of the negotiations.

The acquisition of PLDT followed a failed attempt to gain control of San Miguel Corporation, the Philippines' and one of Asia's premier brewers. That takeover attempt suggests that Mr. Pangilinan's overall objectives may have been less focused than some suggest, and that the priority was acquiring attractive assets in Asia, regardless of sector.

That argument is typical of analysts' perspective of First Pacific and Mr. Pangilinan: decidedly mixed. That didn't change when PLDT was acquired. Some felt that PLDT's dominance of the market and First Pacific's solid history in cellular service bode well; others, that First Pacific had a bad habit of overpaying for projects that were difficult to implement.

However, most business subscribers rejoiced when Mr. Pangilinan gained control of PLDT, confident that he and the sharp group of executives that populate the group's other interests would drag PLDT out of the history books and into the real world.

But soon after the acquisition, warning signs emerged. Most prominent was the news that a PLDT affiliate, cellular provider PilTel, was unable to service its debt of US$898.2 million, which was significantly higher than what First Pacific had thought. No due diligence was conducted before the merger. In February 1999, PLDT announced net revenues that were 86% lower than that of the previous year due to provisions for losses on unpaid bills.

As a result, the media and analysts began to wonder whether the mess PLDT was in when Mr. Pangilinan took over could ever be fixed. Indeed, the frustration associated with that task was increasingly apparent in Mr. Pangilinan's public pronouncements, which had on occasion been both inappropriate and beneath him. An acquaintance told one of his associates once: "Why does Manny seem to be whining all the time?"

To his friends, Mr. Pangilinan has always been very unassuming; unlike many mid-level and senior executives who believe they are important just because they work for a company. So, it was in character when he patiently explained during one interview that what he was trying to accomplish at PLDT had been radically misinterpreted.

Mr. Pangilinan was not trying to repair PLDT, which probably was impossible. He was recreating it.

Two forces, according to Mr. Pangilinan, were driving recreation at PLDT. The first was liberalization. The company was having to learn to compete despite its continued dominance of fixed-line telecommunications. Second was the way people communicate, or more precisely, the Internet. While PLDT's core business was solidly rooted in voice communications, digital communication and data transmission are the future, and a good deal of the present in 2000, too.

Mr. Pangilinan cited work in three areas to illustrate how the company was responding and remaking itself as a result of the impact of liberalization and the new

Internet economy. The first area had to do with the network itself, which presented Mr. Pangilinan with a difficult contradiction. Because of the investment in its core, voice-based network, the company was obviously unable to start with the clean slate that new telecommunications firms have when they start from scratch. On the other hand, it couldn't lag behind, either, particularly with the increasing prevalence of wireless competition and the introduction of fast wireless Internet access later this year by the competition.

So, Mr. Pangilinan was moving to combine network, fixed, and mobile access into a bundled package for customers, or what is called convergence. In addition to infrastructure — PLDT owns Home Cable and Internet service provider Infocom — Mr. Pangilinan wanted to produce content, and was investing in Internet start-ups that would do that.

For customers, the second area, Mr. Pangilinan's value proposition was the best total solution: PLDT intends to provide everything a corporate and individual customer needs in the way of communication, from voice to data to video. Initially, the company was focusing on corporate customers and formed a corporate and large accounts sales group to begin building value-added relationships.

The third area was operations, and an obvious area for improvement. Mr. Pangilinan said that, as in the case of the company's existing network, his intent was to capitalize on the company's strengths while addressing its weaknesses. Billing, human resource practice, and backroom integration were all strengthened.

Like PLDT itself, recreating this organization was a huge story, and a complex one to be sure, exciting as it was challenging. And although Mr. Pangilinan had as many detractors as admirers, both were likely to bet in the long term that he would pull it off. Perhaps not because of his unrelenting focus on core businesses — just his unrelenting focus on succeeding.

For companies falling within the conservative category, making a "vertical" shift or improving their competitiveness is a key strategy (see Figure 5.6). Companies that experience windfall profits must know that their "competitiveness" will not last long. Once the Asian economies recover and Asian currencies strengthen, they will no longer be able to offer competitive prices to world markets. Besides, there is always the threat that more efficient competitors will emerge to offer cheaper prices. Meanwhile, Asian state-owned companies must stop relying on the monopoly granted by the government, especially when the trend is toward more privatization. As the market is deregulated, more efficient foreign competitors will easily win, since they will be able to offer better value to customers.

To ward off these threats, conservative companies must strive to improve efficiency or to acquire other competitive assets, such as building strong brand equity. Singapore Telecom and Hong Kong Telecom are among the few Asian state-owned companies that are efficiently managed in a world-class manner. With their relatively strong financial condition, these companies continue to innovate new ways to improve efficiency and to offer better value to their customers. In the middle of the Asian crisis, both Singapore Telecom and Hong Kong Telecom

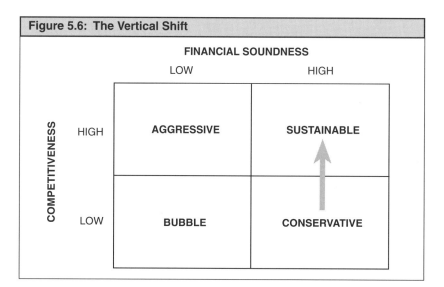

Figure 5.6: The Vertical Shift

continued to improve their interactive PC and interactive TV offerings in their respective markets.[11] Recently, Hong Kong Telecom even sealed an agreement with Microsoft Corporation to further develop interactive PCs in Hong Kong using its islandwide broadband network.

Sustainable Companies

Sustainable companies are those that have strong global competitiveness and good financial management. They usually hold strong competitive assets, which may include strong brand equity, superior economies of scale, committed employees, and innovation. Most of these companies are able to deliver superior value to their customers, shareholders, and employees. Not surprisingly, most of these companies are among the most admired companies in the region. Typically, they employ effective business strategies in the markets in which they operate. On the financial front, they are relatively conservative, evaluate their investments prudently, and have low debt-to-equity ratios. Due to these qualities, these companies are not seriously affected during economic downturns.

A clear example of a sustainable Asian company is Singapore Airlines (SIA).[12] SIA, with a market capitalization of S$20 billion, has the best financial performance in the airline industry. It has consistently posted handsome profits from year to year. In the difficult year of 1998, it managed to record US$603 million in profit from US$4.6 billion revenue. Its growth was organic, not debt-driven. Aeroplanes, for example, were purchased from cash flows without recourse to borrowing. Despite its financial conservatism, the airline was aggressive in marketing and customer service to develop a premium brand and image. For example, when other Asian airlines struggled to survive the crisis, SIA continued to innovate better ways of offering services to its customers. SIA's employees are also among the best in the industry. It has achieved this by training its employees extensively. For example, its stewardesses — the iconic Singapore Girls — are trained over four months, while

Western airlines settle for only two months' training. Not satisfied with being one of the most admired Asian companies, SIA also wants to use the crisis to strengthen its position globally. With zero debt and cash of S$1.6 billion, it is seeking to expand by purchasing stakes in recession-hit regional carriers.

Truly sustainable companies are the ones that do not just enjoy their advantageous position. Instead, they continually scan their business environment in order to exploit other opportunities that will strengthen their already advantageous position, and continually improve themselves internally. They drive themselves through the sustainability loop described in Chapter 2 (see Figure 5.7). Asian companies must strive to become sustainable companies by mastering these loops. Here we describe two Asian companies that have done so.

Building Sustainability at Acer[13]

The Acer Group, Taiwan's largest integrated computer company that manufactures PCs, peripherals, and semiconductors, has undergone a successful "change journey."

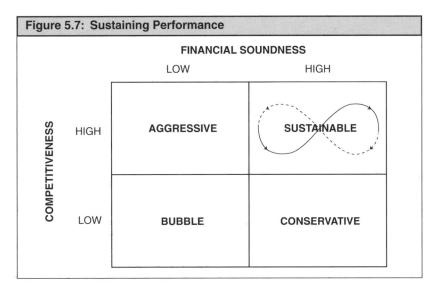

Figure 5.7: Sustaining Performance

The Exploitation Stage

In 1976, with an initial capital of NT$1 million (around US$25,000 at the time), Stan Shih, Acer's legendary founder, along with four co-founders (including his wife, Carolyn Yeh), established Multitech, Acer's forerunner, which mainly manufactured microprocessor machines. During the start-up years, the market for Multitech's offerings was practically non-existent since the general public in Taiwan had no idea what a microprocessor machine was. To overcome this, Multitech had to set up training centers focusing on microprocessor technologies to promote the new concept and cultivate the potential market in Taiwan. They also put out a monthly publication, *The Gardener's Words*, to educate consumers about the technology and applications of microprocessor machines. In this "emergent" stage, no formal management system was put in place, but everyone's goal was clear: to accomplish a long-term and sound development of Taiwan's microprocessor market. Shih, who along with his wife owned a 50% share of the company, served as the "entrepreneurial leader" to reach a goal that seemed lofty at the time. Shih successfully led the company by building a corporate spirit of strong self-initiative among the employees and a culture of mutual trust between the partners and employees.

The Conservation Stage

After passing through the difficult start-up stage, Acer entered into a growth phase in the 1980s. Multitech Industrials Corporation, the first spin-off company, was established in 1981. Acer also set up its first manufacturing plant in the Hsinchu Science Industrial Park, considered by many as Taiwan's "Silicon Valley." In 1986, Acer began to enter a phase of aggressive globalization. It recruited talent, purchased land, and constructed plants worldwide. In 1988, Acer went public on the Taiwan Stock Exchange. Taking advantage of the unprecedented prosperity in the Taiwan stock market, Acer was able to raise enough cash within a short time to embark on the task of globalization. Dr. Leonard Liu, then an IBM vice president, was hired as president of Acer Inc. In this stage, employee morale was at an all-time high and there was great confidence about the future. The company appeared to be at its pinnacle.

The Creative Destruction Stage

In truth, however, Acer's competitiveness was declining. Acer had experienced more than ten years of exceptional growth, but the company also suffered the dysfunctionality fall-outs of fast growth. The risk- and profit-sharing relations between the company and its employees changed. The company's investment policy became too daring and imprudent. In *Me-too is Not My Style*, Shih identified five causes of "business disease" that weakened Acer's structure at the time: too much cash, a gigantic structure, lack of a sense of crisis, slow response, and blurred authority and responsibility.

In 1990, realizing that the company had grown too big, Shih undertook "creative destruction" at Acer. The transformation came in two stages. The first stage was to transform the group organization into several lean and mean autonomous units managed by a cadre of entrepreneurial CEOs. Several hundred employees were laid off. At the company headquarters alone, the staff was cut from 300 to 80. The result was improved overall efficiency and an enhanced sense of proprietorship among the remaining staff. The second stage, in 1992, involved modification of the company's business model as it adopted the decentralized management approach of a "fast-food" operation model and a "client-server" structure.

The Renewal Stage

When the transformation project was implemented, Acer's long-term debt burden surfaced in its financial reports. It was the first time in Acer's history that it had failed to meet its profit target. Shih also had to deal with the remaining employees' low morale. Employees were worried that there might be a second round of lay-offs. As Shih put it, "On one hand, I wanted to maintain a sense of crisis among our employees, but on the other hand, I also had to comfort our employees." After several rounds of lay-offs, however, the situation gradually stabilized. By 1993, the operation began to break even, and as conditions improved, employees began to recognize that the lay-off resolution was correct.

Restarting The Loop

Acer's transformation was successful and yielded good results: Acer managed to break into the ranks of the top ten PC producers in the world. The Acer brand name is also one of the most recognizable international brands from Asia after Sony.

The process of renewal did not stop there. After reaping the benefits of the major restructuring in 1990, Acer once again entered the "creative destruction" stage by undertaking its second major "re-engineering" project in 1998. As a result, while many firms in the region succumbed to the Asian crisis, Acer has been doing relatively well and is ahead on the curve of restructuring.

The Lippo Group: Building Sustainability through Synergy and Conservatism[14]

The Lippo Group has also managed to sustain itself through various stages.

The Exploitation Stage

After achieving great success as the top bank executive in Indonesia (including accomplishing turnarounds of several major banks), in 1976 Dr. Mochtar Riady founded the Lippo Group, a major Indonesian conglomerate focusing on property and financial services. Lippo's name and logo represent Dr. Riady's vision as well as his success. The Chinese words *li* (energy) and *pao* (treasure) capture the essence of his business philosophy: to find the synergy between human endeavor and financial resources. The logo is a stylized graphic rendering of the letters "L" and "P" in a continuous loop whose core simulates the mathematics symbol for infinity and unending growth.

The Lippo Group's big break came when the Indonesian government deregulated the banking sector in October 1988 and sought foreign investment. At the time, Lippo was ready to capitalize on the unprecedented demand for financial services in the big Indonesian market. In 1989, Lippo changed the name of Bank Perniagaan Indonesia, in which Mochtar Riady had bought a 49% stake seven years before, to Lippobank, and merged it with Bank Umum Asia. (The merged entity uses Lippobank as its name.)

The Conservation Stage

Following the deregulation policy, the country's banking industry became much more competitive. In this environment, Lippobank found fertile growth in retail banking, a field in which it could be called the pioneer, attracting deposits from Indonesia's growing pool of middle-class professionals and meshing with the government's desire to mobilize domestic savings to reduce foreign debt. Lippobank opened branches at a breakneck pace, spending large sums on marketing. It was run along American lines, with sophisticated technology and professional management. It brought banking to small depositors by developing "bank-mindedness," offering simplified procedures, efficient service, and a convenient branch network, all of which allowed premium pricing.

While it was aggressive in marketing, Lippobank practiced conservative finance. It avoided currency risks by staying out of foreign exchange dealings except for covering commercial trade transactions. It concentrated on servicing distributors and traders (rather than manufacturers), who would not be adversely affected by economic conditions. In addition, it focused on consumer banking for deposits.

Banking is not Lippo's only business. Through the 1980s, the Lippo Group acquired interests in a variety of businesses: investment banking, insurance, brokerage, infrastructure and urban development, IT, and manufacturing (textiles, automotive parts, consumer products). But banking remains the cornerstone of Lippo's Asia-Pacific strategy, because banks bring image, reputation, human resources, and an earnings base that allows exploration of other opportunities. Above all, banking brings networks.

In 1984, Lippo acquired the Hong Kong Chinese Bank, a sleepy retail institution in Hong Kong. In 1985, younger son, Stephen Riady, came to Hong Kong to represent Lippo's interests. Hong Kong is the group's base for investment banking, insurance, and tourism activities, which Mochtar Riady saw as significant growth areas for Southeast Asia in the latter part of the 1990s. Each area grew through alliances. For example, Lippo's merchant banking unit formed joint syndicates with Japanese banks. Its Hong Kong-based international insurance business has many joint ventures with Tokyo Mutual Life, Fuji Fire and Marine, and Alexander & Alexander, an American insurance broker and risk management specialist. And through its ownership in the Hong Kong Chinese Bank, Lippo developed a relationship with China Resources (Holdings), Beijing's premier international trading group and one of the largest mainland enterprises in Hong Kong. China Resources' range of businesses is similar to that of the giant Jardine Matheson Group. The deals between Lippo and its allies in Hong Kong quickly moved Lippo into a strategic position in China. In 1992, Lippo announced plans for a joint venture bank in Shenzhen, China, adjacent to Hong Kong. In that same year, Lippo also created public holding companies for Hong Kong and Indonesia, giving Hong Kong corporate prominence as a second headquarters and a springboard to China.

Since 1992, the Lippo Group has seriously entered into two other businesses in Indonesia, property and insurance, which are expected to be its main pillars. As in the banking sector, the Lippo Group has taken many innovative steps. In property, it is fighting against the iron law of property, developing two satellite cities in the outskirts of Jakarta, Karawaci and Cikarang. These two cities are equipped with shopping and recreational centers, a business area, hotel, hospital, school, and university. Meanwhile, in the insurance business, the Lippo Group, through Lippo Life, has applied marketing strategies commonly used in the consumer goods industry. Lippo makes use of integrated marketing strategies, starting from segmentation, and moving through targeting and positioning to branding. Through these efforts, the Lippo Group has provoked the Indonesian people to be insurance-minded. Mochtar Riady believes that capital mobilization, necessary for Indonesia's development programs, can be supported by insurance — along with taxes, banking, and capital markets.

The Creative Destruction and Renewal Stages

Having anticipated that Indonesia's banking industry would face serious problems at some stage, Mochtar Riady has taken a conservative stance since 1993 by not expanding Lippobank too quickly. As a result, Lippobank had a lower profile than some other private banks.

In October 1996, the Lippo Group restructured its financial business in Indonesia, making Lippo Securities the holding company with Lippo Life as its direct subsidiary and Lippobank as its indirect subsidiary. Lippo Securities is an operating company with interests in securities, retail brokerage, and investment banking. The consolidating move created a synergy among its financial businesses. Lippo's integrated marketing strategies in insurance made Lippo Life not only an insurer with the highest growth rate in Indonesia, but also an insurer with the strongest balance sheet in the country.

At the end, both Lippo Group's conservatism in developing Lippobank and its restructuring efforts to create synergy among its business units have made the Lippo Group relatively immune to the banking crisis in Indonesia. In 1998, Lippobank was one of the few banks in Indonesia that managed to record strong operating profits. Even though by late 1998 Lippobank had succumbed to the extended crisis (joining the state-sponsored recapitalization program), Lippo Group as a whole remains strong. The Group is ready to inject 20% of the funds necessary for the recapitalization program.

According to Mochtar Riady, there are currently three categories of banks in Indonesia: banks that were already in trouble prior to the crisis; banks that are in trouble due to the crisis; and banks that have survived the crisis. Aside from the solid performance of Lippo Group as a whole, Lippobank belongs in the third category, which is a truly great accomplishment considering the severity of the Indonesian banking crisis.

Conclusion

Asian companies have been impacted by the Asian crisis in different ways. Some faced dangers, while others saw opportunities. No matter how they were affected, Asian companies cannot stand still. They must strive to become sustainable companies by adopting sound business strategies that will enable them to respond appropriately to the increasingly dynamic business environment.

1   Andersen Consulting, "Creating the Breakaway Advantage," April 1998.
2   *The Wall Street Journal 1998 Asian Economic Survey.*
3   Andersen Consulting, op. cit.
4   Yuji Akaba, Florian Budde, and Jungkiu Choi, "A cure for sick *chaebol*," *The Asian Wall Street Journal*, November 19, 1998.
5   See "Reinventing an Asian brand," *Asiaweek*, May 14, 1999.
6   See "Daewoo's incredible shrinking act," *Fortune*, May 24, 1999.
7   Yuji Akaba et al., "A cure for sick *chaebol*,"op. cit.
8   See Taufik, "Indofood's transformation into a multinational corporation," *MarkPlus Quarterly*, Vol. 2, No. 1 (1999).
9   "Good Companies in Bad Times," *The Asian Wall Street Journal's Asian Economic Survey 1997–1998.*
10 Hilsenrath, Jon E., "Hong Kong's First Pacific buys 27% stake in PLDT," *The Wall Street Journal Interactive*, November 25, 1998, Internet edition.

11   Andersen Consulting, "Horizon 2010: Technological Trends in Asia," September 1998.

12   Summarized from S. Jayasankaran, "Gaining speed: Singapore Airlines expands its lead as rivals fall back," *Far Eastern Economic Review*, July 1, 1999, pp. 48–49.

13   This section draws heavily on Stan Shih, *Me-too is Not My Style* (Taipei: Acer Foundation, 1996).

14   This section draws heavily on Taufik, "Competing in the new financial services industry: Interview with Lippo Group's Mochtar Riady," *MarkPlus Quarterly*, Vol. 2, No. 1 (1999).

A Winning Business Strategy Model for Asian Companies

6

Prior to the Asian crisis, everyone wanted to do business in Asia. Many companies operating in the region exploited the opportunities it provided, from its favorable demographics to its consistently high economic growth. "Stable" government leaderships in most Asian countries had also created a desirable macroeconomic stability. Inflation had been kept low. Currencies had been maintained at a stable level. In this benign business environment, Asian companies had been growing and expanding aggressively. Many Asian companies, especially the conglomerates, had relied much on connections, and little effort was directed toward building strong management systems.

When the Asian crisis struck, the business environment in Asia was thrown into turmoil. *Change drivers* — such as technology, macroeconomic conditions, political/legal conditions, market conditions, and consumers' behavior and preferences — all changed with unimaginable velocity. Today, Asian companies have no other choice but to revamp their old ways of doing business. Merely relying on connections will no longer work. They must pay close attention to the direction and velocity of the changes presented by the crisis. They must study changes in their business environment, competitors, and customers. They must also evaluate their policies and review their internal strengths in order to be able to identify both opportunities and threats. And last but not least, they must reassess their management systems. With these efforts, Asian companies will be able to anticipate changes more appropriately.

Asian companies will need to reformulate their *strategic business design*. This is the *strategic blueprint* for the company to win the market and maintain growth. In formulating a strategic blueprint, companies should follow the sustainable marketing enterprise model. The model does not present a unique prescription of how companies should manage their businesses, since there is no single prescription that all companies should follow. Rather, the model offers a systematic methodology that a particular company can apply to assess its starting conditions, its major opportunities, and its strengths and weaknesses, in order to set an effective strategy.

The sustainable marketing enterprise model consists of three interrelated sub-models. The first sub-model, *sustainability*, has been covered extensively in Chapters 2 and 5. We have shown that while short-term survival efforts are crucial, Asian companies need to move toward becoming a sustainable company in order to win not only in the short term, but also in the long term. More importantly, a truly sustainable company is one that continually reviews and adjusts its business strategy so that it can respond appropriately to its ever-changing business environment.

The next question is: How can Asian companies determine the right strategy in the face of the ever-changing market? The answer lies in the *marketing* sub-model. Marketing, which is commonly interpreted as a departmental function within an organization, here is interpreted as "dealing with the market."

The third sub-model, *enterprise*, consists of several frameworks and tools that will guide an organization to become a truly sustainable enterprise.

In the rest of this chapter, we will explain the marketing and enterprise sub-models.

The Marketing Sub-model

Within the marketing sub-model, there are three parts: outlook, architecture, and scorecard. Together, they form the *strategic marketing flow* (see Figure 6.1). Let's look at each part in detail.

The Strategic Business Outlook in the "New Asia"

The first task is to develop a picture of the strategic business outlook in the "New Asia." Asia's restructuring will, in effect, create new sets of challenges for companies operating in the region. The 4Cs Diamond tool looks at the outlook of four elements of the business environment: change, competition, customer, and company (see Figure 6.2). We have already examined change in Chapter 3. Here we will examine the other three elements (competition, customer, and company).

Competition

Changes — triggered by technological, economic, political/legal, sociocultural, and market forces — serve as "value-migrators"[1] within an industry. These changes influence all the players within the industry. They alter the competitive landscape. It is therefore imperative for a company to closely monitor competitors' activities in the hope of creating the right strategy. A company must be able to identify competitors who are likely to be stronger or weaker, or even to drop out of the

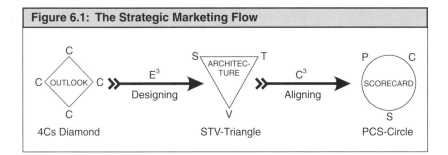

Figure 6.1: The Strategic Marketing Flow

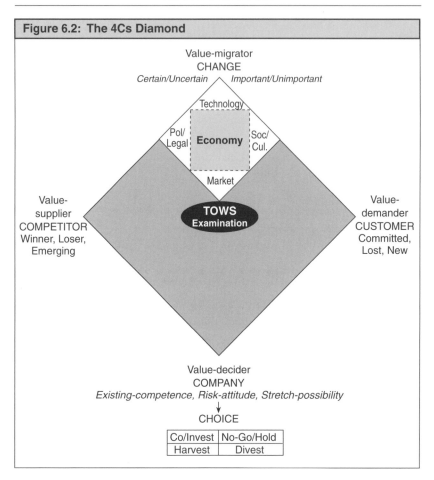

Figure 6.2: The 4Cs Diamond

Value-migrator
CHANGE
Certain/Uncertain   *Important/Unimportant*

Technology

Pol/Legal | **Economy** | Soc/Cul.

Market

TOWS Examination

Value-supplier
COMPETITOR
Winner, Loser, Emerging

Value-demander
CUSTOMER
Committed, Lost, New

Value-decider
COMPANY
Existing-competence, Risk-attitude, Stretch-possibility

CHOICE

Co/Invest	No-Go/Hold
Harvest	Divest

competition, as a result of the "value-migration." It should also pay attention to potential new entrants. By considering the competitive landscape, a company will know how tough the competition is likely to be.

Several key issues to address when creating the competitive profile include:

- Who are the current and future competitors?
- How are competitors performing, and what capabilities drive their performance?
- How does each of the competitors position itself in the marketplace?
- What is the basis of competition?

In general, the competitive landscape in Asia will shift from the dominance of private Asian companies toward the dominance of multinational companies (MNCs). Prior to the crisis, most private Asian companies were "protected" by the state-led development policies of Asian governments. As a result, these companies grew in confidence and borrowed extensively to fund their aggressive expansion. Meanwhile, MNCs had been facing restrictions in various Asian markets. For example, foreign ownership had been restricted to minority control in most Asian countries.

When the Asian crisis struck, the situation changed almost 180 degrees. Many private Asian companies faced ballooning debt burdens and were forced to restructure their businesses. Some companies that seemed potent prior to the crisis even faced bankruptcy or lost ownership of their businesses. MNCs, on the other hand, saw many opportunities to expand their presence in Asia. Due to Asia's indebtedness to international bodies such as the IMF, governments of crisis-hit Asian countries — in particular, Indonesia, Thailand, and South Korea — have been forced to open up their markets more. In Thailand's telecommunications industry, for example, foreign partners are now allowed to own more than a 25% share of joint ventures.[2] In Thailand's banking industry, the government increased foreign ownership limits from 25% to 100% for the next ten years.[3] As a result, MNCs are seizing opportunities to take market leadership in various Asian industries. MNCs with large financial resources are able to purchase controling shares, or even to wholly acquire local companies at very cheap prices. Furthermore, Asian governments (especially Indonesia and Thailand) are accelerating privatization programs to fund state-budget deficits.[4] This gives MNCs a further opportunity to purchase stakes in many state-owned enterprises that previously enjoyed monopolies in their countries. Chapter 7 will discuss in more detail how multinationals can take advantage of the opportunities available to them.

Customer

In a period of recession, consumers generally go through several stages in adjusting their purchasing patterns:[5]

- At first they maintain their old spending pattern, refusing to take their real-income loss seriously.
- As things get worse, they cut certain items from their budget and search for less expensive goods.
- At a further point, they get angry and blame certain forces for the economic downturn — big businesses, unions, and the government.
- Later still, they start despairing of the situation and resign themselves to their lower standard of living.

The economic crisis that befell Asia has changed Asian consumers' buying behavior. As their purchasing power significantly eroded, consumers became more value-oriented in selecting products and services.[6] Consumers based their purchasing decisions not just on quality, but also on price. In the pre-crisis era, Asians tended to be quality-oriented. During the economic crisis, they moved from being quality-driven to value-driven. And the former value-driven consumers moved toward being price-driven.

The change in Asian consumers' behavior is revealed by studies conducted in several Southeast Asian countries after the economic crisis (see Box 6.1). What is interesting is that those customers who had been quality-oriented prior to the crisis still consider quality as important, although their purchasing power has led them to make some value or price substitutions. It should be noted that the consumer behavior studies presented in Box 6.1 are general in nature. Every company should monitor the specific change in consumers' behavior in their particular country and industry. Many Asian companies need to change their assumptions about customer behavior in order to adjust their strategies.

Box 6.1

Consumer Behavior Studies in Indonesia, Malaysia, and the Philippines

Changes in consumer behavior in Indonesia
The economic crisis in Indonesia remains very serious today. The older generation sees it as worse than the crisis they experienced three decades earlier. And the younger generation never anticipated that they would experience rationed shopping and queuing to obtain basic food supplies.

Among the lower economic levels, food was a two-meal-a-day event. To have rice on the table was considered a luxury. Tapioca was more common. Children had to drop out of school because they were barely fed, much less be able to pay for transportation and school supplies. Work and food were scarce, and there were no savings to rely on. It is no wonder that sporadic looting and demonstrations have occurred.

Those in higher economic segments no longer thought of taking an overseas vacation. They made do with trips to the local resorts, which were no longer busy spots. For foreigners, Indonesia is a paradise for branded goods; but for the locals, branded goods were no longer on their shopping lists. Savings were kept for potentially worse situations. In general, people spent less time outside the home. While safety was a big concern, spending time outside the house meant "eating" into one's budget. Therefore, there was less window-shopping, less eating out, less shopping for clothes, fewer visits to the cinema, and fewer trips out of town. With more time at home, family members had more time to spend and communicate with one another. Watching TV together became a more common pastime.

Of all the family members, babies received the best attention in terms of food consumption. Mothers were aware that the most important life stage is the early years and so they didn't compromise when buying infant's milk. Switching brands or types may cause indigestion, which would create even more problems if the child needed medical help.

The same applies for personal skincare and shampoo products. Switching to other brands may cause negative side-effects. The best that the female consumer could do was to use smaller amounts. Cooking oil were another product where consumers maintained brands but reduced their usage. Among those in the lower economic class, the use of milk products if not for children was reduced, and many stopped consuming milk entirely. Products in the "stop usage" segment, such as chocolate, snacks, and cereals, were considered secondary; thus, the absence of these from the dining table was accepted. Those in the quadrant of "switch to value-for-money brands" saw these products as functional, and therefore choosing a cheaper brand that could fulfill the same purpose would help the family budget. Box Figure 6.1 illustrates consumers' coping mechanisms by product category.

Changes in consumer behavior in Malaysia

The most immediate impact of the economic crisis in Malaysia was increasing prices. Prices in most categories increased, ranging from about 10% to 15%. Malaysians adjusted by cutting down on expenses.

People in the higher income group, who were hit by losses in the stock market and property market, cut down on luxury items such as overseas trips and expensive branded goods. However, having accumulated wealth in the past, they still had sufficient savings to fall back on.

Most Malaysians coped by reducing expenses by, say, eating out less, making fewer weekend trips, and doing less window-shopping. They spent more time at home with the family, watching TV, reading, and listening to music.

Box Figure 6.1: Coping Strategies by Product Categories – Indonesia

Cash Cows (Maintain brand and usage)	Elephants (Maintain brand, reduce usage)
Infant milk Deodorant Talcum powder Toothpaste Skincare Sanitary protection Hand and body lotion Shampoo Tea/coffee	Cooking oil Instant noodles Facial soap Skincare Canned fish/meat Margarine/butter Coffee Carbonated soft drinks Chocolate/candy Tissue Milk powder Vitamin/food supplement
Chocolate RTD milk Breakfast cereals Carbonated soft drinks Sweetened condensed milk Baby cereals Milk powder Imported fruits	Toilet soap Detergent Sanitary protection Toilet paper Insecticides House cleanser Tissue
Dinosaurs (Stop usage)	Chameleons (Switch to "value-for-money" brands)

The crisis has made some people reflect about life and the past. They realized that life prior to the crisis consisted of many unnecessary indulgences. This phenomenon is not dissimilar to what happened in Japan during the bursting of the "bubble economy" in the late 1980s. Box Figure 6.2 illustrates Malaysian consumers' coping mechanisms by product category.

Where babies' diet and nutrition was concerned — for example, infant's milk — mothers made no compromises. Skincare products, particularly moisturizers, were also items Malaysian females remained loyal to for fear of side-effects should they change their brand. They retained the same brand and some reduced their usage. Personal care products such as toothpaste and deodorant also survived the crisis. Instant coffee was either maintained or reduced, as consumers placed great importance on its taste and hence, were reluctant to opt for cheaper brands. Products such as carbonated soft drinks, chocolate, and snacks were considered frills in these times of economic adversity. Consumption was either reduced (but keeping to the same brand among the higher income group) or stopped altogether (among the lower income group).

Although carbonated soft drinks increased in price by a mere 3% over the previous year, the sales volume decreased by 12%, suggesting that consumers not only look at the price increase but also question how necessary

Box Figure 6.2: Coping Strategies by Product Categories – Malaysia

Cash Cows (Maintain brand and usage)	Elephants (Maintain brand, reduce usage)
Infant milk Milk powder Instant coffee Skincare Toothpaste Deodorant	Diapers Carbonated soft drinks Haircare Skincare Snacks Coffee/tea/hot beverage Chocolate Toothbrush Ice cream
Chocolate Snacks Cereals Carbonated soft drinks Fresh milk Air-fresheners Body shampoo Floor cleaner	Dishwashing liquid Detergent Floor cleaner Toilet paper Diapers Toothpaste Cooking oil
Dinosaurs (Stop usage)	Chameleons (Switch to "value-for-money" brands)

the item is. Another possible reason for the reduction in consumption of carbonated soft drinks was the government's campaign to encourage people to consume less sugar for health reasons.

The vulnerable categories that are subjected to price competition tend to be mainly household cleaning products, be it detergents, dishwashing products, or floor cleaners. This behavior seems to cut across income groups. The reasons could well be that such products are viewed as functional and lack the emotional attachment of skincare and other products. These "chameleon" products are especially vulnerable when they are only ingredients — for example, cooking oil. Hence, using a cheaper brand is seen to have a minimal effect on the end product.

Perceived luxury items such as fresh milk and body shampoo, to which consumers have "traded up" from milk powder and toilet soaps in recent years, suffered. Their consumption dropped and people were reverting to what they used in the past.

Products with volume increases include instant noodles, cooking oil, and canned sardines — probably due to the return to home-cooking, as eating-out were reduced to save on expenses. Another category that registered growth was household cleaning products, with floor cleaners and dishwashing products on the rise, no doubt brought about by more home-cooking.

Changes in consumer behavior in the Philippines

In a nationwide survey conducted by A.C. Nielsen (Philippines) on how housewives coped with the economic crisis, 75% of respondents reported that their economic situation was worse or a lot worse than it was a year earlier. The situation was worse because commodity prices had risen. The national retail audit showed that most goods increased in price. The biggest price increases had been for throat relievers, cleaners, shampoos, toilet soaps, and "feel good" commodities such as deodorants and facial care products. Food items, though, have not become as expensive, except perhaps for milk and milk-derived products.

No matter how bad the turn in the economy, however, Filipino housewives, even if they found life more difficult, rarely blamed the economic crisis. Rather, they viewed their difficulties as the result of many factors; the economic crisis was just one of them.

Filipino housewives tend to find life still manageable despite the hard times, because for them, there are still ways to get relief. In fact, the hard times are even seen as being good for the soul, because they force a person to focus on *real* needs as opposed to *imagined* needs. Some people cope by viewing their economic distress from a spiritual perspective.

The focus groups on coping behavior unearthed three ways in which budgets are adapted:

- Expense items for food, electricity, and so on, and, for some meticulous consumers, even a fund for emergencies and obligatory social expenses such as birthday gifts for relatives and friends.
- Differentiating between recurring expenses, such as transportation and lunches at work, and one-time expenses, such as monthly payments for a car or house, or pager bills.
- Segmenting expenses by family member, especially among families with very young children. Couples prepare their budget according to their baby's needs. These include the baby's formula, medicines, and diapers. Then they have a separate budget for themselves and other family members, and then a budget for common expenses like the house rent.

Another way that Filipino housewives coped was in the allocation of items. There are several strategies used:

- Reducing consumption by reducing either the amount used per occasion or the frequency of usage.
- Substitution strategy.
- Trading down to cheaper brands.
- Stopping usage altogether.
- Extending or prolonging usage.

Box Figure 6.3 shows some of the items and strategies used by Filipino housewives.

Box Figure 6.3: Coping Strategies by Product Categories – The Philippines	
Cash Cows (Maintain brand and usage)	**Elephants** (Maintain brand, reduce usage)
Infant fomula Baby food and cereals Disposable diapers Toothpaste Shampoo Bath soap	Ice cream Hair conditioner Cosmetics Fragrance Home cleaners Waxes Insecticides
Air fresheners Bread spread Milk products	Toilet paper Detergents Cooking oil
Dinosaurs (Stop usage)	**Chameleons** (Switch to "value-for-money" brands)

Source: European Society for Opinion and Marketing Research (ESOMAR), *From A Thundering Roar to A Simpering Meow: Understanding Sentiments of Indonesians, Malaysians, and Filipinos during the Economic Crisis, 1998.* Summarized by permission of © ESOMAR®, Amsterdam, The Netherlands (www.esomar.nl).

Company

After observing *change*, *competition*, and *customer*, Asian companies may then see prospects for *sustainability*. A company must analyze three issues: its existing core competencies, risk attitude, and stretch possibilities.

In assessing its core competencies, a company must ask:

- Are its core competencies still adequate in dealing with the new situation?
- Are its core competencies unique?
- Will its core competencies fulfill the needs, wants, and expectations of customers in the future?

The company must also assess its risk attitude. Depending on the risk and return it is willing to take, a company can be categorized as a risk-avoider, risk-seeker, or risk-taker (see Figure 6.3). In the pre-crisis era, most Asian companies were aggressive risk-takers. In a crisis companies should evaluate their risk attitude by exercising more prudence in expanding their operations.

After determining its core competencies and risk attitude, a company can then explore its stretch possibilities. If it requires

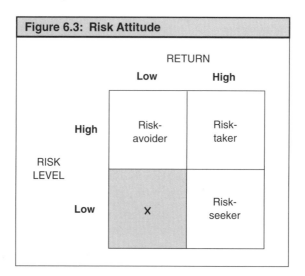

176

new competencies, there are three approaches: develop the competence internally; "buy" the new competence through mergers and acquisitions; or form alliances with other parties who have the competence.

A TOWS (threats-opportunities-weaknesses-strengths) analysis can then be conducted. Based on this analysis, the company can then choose from several options: *go/invest, no-go/hold, harvest,* or *divest*. A *divest* decision means that, after studying its conditions and external environments, the company feels that it can no longer sustain its existence; therefore, it should get out of business by selling the business or liquidating the company's assets. A *harvest* decision means that the company will not invest further in the business. Instead, it will improve its cash flow by reducing expenses without causing sales to fall too much. The *no-go/hold* decision means that the company should maintain its strategy and avoid radical change. Finally, the *go/invest* decision means that the company feels comfortable moving in new investment directions. In this case, the company should revise its strategic business architecture and enterprise model.

Semen Gresik Group (SGG), Indonesia's largest cement producer, serves as a good illustration of a company that responded appropriately to its changing business landscape.[7] In September 1998, SGG established a strategic alliance with Cemex, one of the largest global cement companies. This measure was taken following the decision by the Indonesian government to sell part of the shares of SGG, which had good performance and manageable foreign exchange loans, to Cemex in order to finance Indonesia's restructuring efforts.

This strategic alliance created a momentum for SGG's corporate renewal. As a company whose world-class product was already distributed in a number of Asian countries, SGG had long dreamed of becoming a strong regional player. Its plan was linked with the realization of AFTA in 2003 and APEC liberalization in 2020. SGG had even made preparations in several areas, including augmenting its production capacity by utilizing the latest available technology. Although the crisis that broke out in mid-1997 has had some adverse effects on the company, such as declining domestic demand and a rising debt burden, SGG still has the basic competence to realize its vision. Its domestic and overseas marketing coverage encompasses almost all provinces in Indonesia, a number of Asian countries such as Bangladesh, Sri Lanka, Singapore, and Myanmar, and some African countries. SGG, like other cement producers in Asia, was already a low-cost cement producer in the pre-crisis era; the drop in the exchange rate has made its products even more competitive in the international market. Its production is also supported by modern equipment, which enables it to produce high-quality cements. The only factors that have prevented SGG from becoming a major regional player are limited capital, global network, and IT capacity. That's why when Cemex, a global cement company with strong capital outlay, global network, and IT, decided to purchase SGG's stakes, SGG saw this as an opportunity to realize its long-term plan to become one of the leading players in Asia.

The strategic alliance was a smart and daring decision. It was a smart decision because at the time the alliance was forged, Indonesia, SGG's main market, had not fully recovered from the crisis. It was a daring decision because it transformed SGG's orientation from a company formerly almost entirely inward-looking, because of the large size of the domestic market, to one adopting a significantly outward-looking attitude as reflected in its seriousness about engaging in the new business landscape.

Using 4Cs and TOWS analysis, a company can get a picture of its prospects in the future. In order to align all of its activities with its new vision, the company needs a clear directive, which aims at consolidating the understanding and implementation of the corporate value, corporate strategy, and corporate tactics. The directive is stated in an activity system called the *strategic business triangle system* (see Figure 6.4). The strategic business triangle system contains three elements — brand, positioning, and differentiation — which, respectively, are the "core" elements of corporate value, corporate strategy, and corporate tactics.

As shown in Figure 6.4, brand, positioning, and

differentiation in the strategic business triangle should be integrated and support each other. A positioning is a promise that the company makes to its customers. The promise should be appropriately differentiated. This, in turn, can generate a strong brand. A strong brand supports the positioning. If this intertwining process runs smoothly, then all three components will support each other just like a rolling snowball: the longer it rolls, the bigger its impact.

To implement the concepts effectively, the strategic business triangle should be supported by various applicable programs. These programs consist of three groups: building focus programs, building capacity programs, and building franchise programs. The first program relates to corporate strategy; the second relates to corporate tactic; and the third deals with corporate value.

The strategic business triangle can then be translated into a more detailed strategic business architecture. The formation of strategic business architecture is aimed at making all the

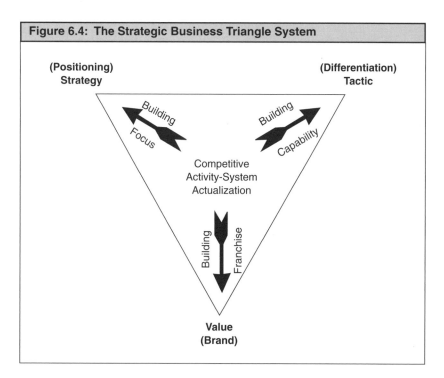

Figure 6.4: The Strategic Business Triangle System

company's business activities systematic, integrated, and comprehensive in facing the turbulent, unpredictable, and uncertain business environment. The strategic business architecture will cover all of the company's activities and, to a greater extent, give direction and guidelines for the company's maneuvering in both domestic and global markets.

Strategic business architecture consists of nine core elements. As shown in Figure 6.5, these nine core elements are: segmentation, targeting, positioning, differentiation, marketing mix, selling, brand, service, and process. The first three elements — segmentation, targeting, and positioning — jointly determine a corporate strategy. Selling, marketing mix and differentiation, constitute a corporate tactic. Brand, service, and process jointly constitute a corporate value. While strategy aims to win the "mind share," value aims to win the "heart share" and tactic to win the "market share."

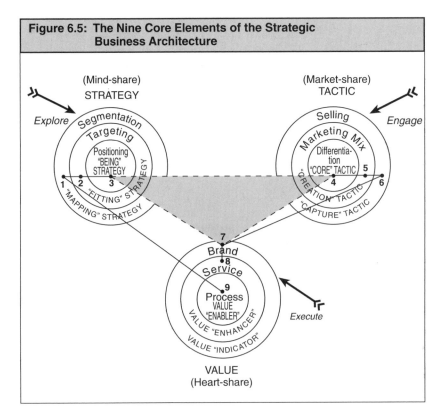

Figure 6.5: The Nine Core Elements of the Strategic Business Architecture

We will now look more carefully at the components of corporate strategy, corporate tactics, and corporate value.

Corporate Strategy

In an article entitled "What is strategy?" Michael Porter defines strategy as "not what is to be done, but rather a limit on what cannot be done in order to make everything go in the same direction."[8] Michael Hamlin, author of *Asia's Best*, also says that "focus and core competence lie at the heart of a firm's competitiveness."[9] He further argues that focus and core competence are complementary, as one reinforces the other. Companies may become focused as a result of the development of a core competence, and core competence may evolve from a focused strategy.

In the same way, the elements of strategy — which consist of segmentation, targeting, and positioning — serve as the limits of what a company cannot do in order to build and sustain its competitiveness. This concept is particularly recommended for Asian conglomerates that had diversified their businesses blindly in the pre-crisis era, often into areas where they did not have strong competencies. In the "New Asia," where sustainable competitiveness is crucial, these companies must formulate a more focused strategy.

A company must first explore the market by doing segmentation (the "mapping" strategy), which is to identify clusters of similar buyers in the market. Targeting (the "fitting" strategy) is the next step; it is the choosing of the segments the company wants to serve. Then, it must establish a clear positioning (the "being" strategy), which is the winning of a place in the buyers' mind.

Segmentation

Because of limited resources, a company cannot offer all the products that a market might want. It must distinguish the different need groups in the market. Markets can be segmented by geographic, demographic, psychographic (lifestyle), and behavioral variables. Segmentation using geographic or demographic variables is easier to conduct, but psychographic and behavioral variables can give a more accurate picture of the specific buyer groups.

Targeting

In choosing the right target market, a company should use four criteria: segment size, segment growth, the company's competitive advantage, and the company's competitive situation. Based on these criteria, it must select market segments that "fit" with its objectives and resources and where it can achieve superior performance.

Positioning

In determining its positioning, a company should pay attention to four considerations:

- The positioning should fit with the company's strengths.
- The positioning should be clearly different than the competitors' positioning.
- The positioning should be positively perceived (liked and believable) by customers.
- The positioning should be sustainable for some time.

It is important to stress here that positioning is a "promise" that a company makes to its customers. To build credibility for the positioning, it is necessary for the company to fulfill its promise by way of building a strong differentiation. Otherwise, the company will "over-promise, but under-deliver."

Corporate Tactics

The realization of strategy and value is *tactic*, which directs how a company engages itself in the marketplace, where the real battle occurs. There are three elements of tactic: differentiation, marketing mix, and selling. Differentiation is the "core" tactic, since it is the basis for attracting actual or potential customers to buy a company's offerings instead of its competitors' offerings. Differentiation has to be "translated" into marketing mix. Marketing mix is called the "creation" tactic, since a company can adjust its elements (product, price, place, and promotion) creatively to differentiate the company's offerings. Finally, selling is the "capture" tactic, since it is the only element that "captures" the value back from the market through the creation of business transactions.

Differentiation

A company can differentiate its offerings in three dimensions: content (what to offer), context (how to offer), and infrastructure (the enabler to offer). Content is the tangible part; it is what a company actually offers to its customers. Context is the intangible part; it relates to the company's efforts to help its customers "perceive" its offerings differently (compared to competitors' offerings). The last dimension, infrastructure, consists of the technology and/or people to support the content and context differentiation.

Marketing mix

To make differentiation effective, the company must develop an appropriate marketing mix. The marketing mix covers four components commonly known as the 4Ps — product, price, place, and promotion. Product and price are the *offer* components. Place and promotion are the *access* components. To develop an effective marketing mix, offer and access (to customers) should be designed in an integrated manner.

Selling

The differentiation and marketing mix will need to be supported by an adequate concept of selling. A company may select one of several selling approaches that suits its target market, whether quality-oriented, value-oriented, or price-oriented. For the quality-oriented segment, a company may use a solution selling approach. The role of the company's salesforce is to proactively identify problems faced by customers and present solutions. For the value-oriented segment, the company may use a benefit-selling approach, by offering customers a high-quality product at a competitive price. For the price-oriented segment, a company may offer a stripped-down version of the product at the lowest possible price.

Corporate Value

A company's ability to retain or acquire customers largely depends on its ability to generate value and customer satisfaction. Value can be measured as "total get" divided by "total give" (from the customer's point of view). "Total get" consists of all the benefits that customers receive (for example, the product's functional benefits, convenience, and so on), while "total give" is what the customer must give up to obtain the benefits (for example, price of products, transportation expenses, and so on).

There are five generic "value strategies."[10] First, a company can choose to give *more* benefits to customers for *less* costs compared to its competitors (*more for less*). Second, it can give *more* benefits to customers for the *same* costs compared to its competitors (*more for same*). Third, it can choose to give the *same* benefits for *less* costs (*same for less*). Fourth, it can give *more* benefits for *more* costs (*more for more*). Finally, it can also choose to give *less* benefits for *less* costs (*less for less*).

The core element of value is brand, since it serves as the *value indicator* of a company or a product. The value of the brand, however, is enhanced through excellent service. Thus, while brand is the value indicator, service is the *value enhancer*. The last (but not least) element of value is process as the *value enabler*.

Brand
Building strong brands is crucial for sustaining Asian companies' long-term competitiveness. However, excepting Japanese companies, very few Asian companies have the will, resources, and experience to build global brands. Asian companies may have the capabilities to manufacture various

products at very competitive costs, but often for Western clients who put their labels on the goods.

Some efforts have already been undertaken to promote Asian brands. Inspired by General Electric, South Korea's LG Group is mounting a worldwide effort to become one of the first global Asian brands outside Japan.[11] An advertising campaign appearing in international business publications introduces LG to the rest of the world with the tagline: "It's nice to meet you." The ads show off the company's far-flung operations, stretching from electronics-design offices in Dublin to semiconductor operations in Sunnyvale, California. The company does business in more than 120 countries, and almost every product produced by LG's 48 companies will be re-branded with its newly designed logo.

In Taiwan, the Board of Foreign Trade headed an effort to build brand names by funneling low-interest bank loans to companies that want to build up their brand names.[12] Through a fund set up in 1991, the government has guaranteed US$46 million in loans from banks to 29 companies, which use the money to improve their advertising, marketing, packaging, design, and customer services.

Although the two above-mentioned examples are noteworthy, many other Asian companies need to make greater commitments to build their own brands and learn from the successful brand-building experiences of their American and European counterparts.

A corporate brand, as expressed in the company's name and logo, is a value indicator to the customers and prospects. It indicates the company's attributes, benefits, values, culture, and personality.[13] Building and maintaining brand equity are not easy tasks and require significant investment. For example, companies in the United States spend between US$100 million and US$300 million annually on brand advertising alone.[14] Brand-building, however, requires more than designing a logo and aggressive advertising campaigns. The brand should be supported by the appropriate service and process excellence.

Service

A corporate brand would be positively perceived by customers if it is supported by suitable service. Nowadays, service has become a paradigm. Service is not just after-sales service, before-sales service, or even a business category. Service should be written with a capital "S," which means that *every* business is actually in a service business.

Process

No matter how good a company's other eight elements, it will be useless unless there is a good process to support them. A company must deal with three cross-disciplinary processes, which are: supply-chain management, market-based asset management, and new product development.[15]

The objective of supply-chain management is to minimize overhead costs across the company's supply chain. The objective of market-based asset management is to optimize all components of market-based assets — such as knowledge of the business environment condition; and relationships between a company and its customers, suppliers, distributors, and retailers. Finally, new product development is aimed at producing innovative products and production processes to achieve the highest level of efficiency.

Winning Strategies in the Asian Crisis

The changes in consumer behavior as a result of the economic crisis demand corresponding, often fundamental, changes in marketing strategy.[16] Many companies, from retailers to hospitals, have begun to restructure their services in an effort to maintain quality and continue to offer competitive prices to the consumer. In order to trim prices in response to the decline in consumer buying power, companies have started to cut logistical and other overhead costs. Companies, especially those producing consumer goods, are also making changes to their product mix, and repackaging their products in smaller sizes.

Unilever in Indonesia, for instance, has repackaged its Magnum ice cream into a smaller-sized product with a more affordable price. Meanwhile, many companies in the service industry have started listening closely to consumers through various retention and loyalty programs. The shrinking Asian market has forced many companies to expand their horizons and seek new markets elsewhere. Acer, for instance, is redirecting its efforts toward the Chinese, South Asian, and Australian markets. The national sentiment that has intensified throughout Asia as a result of the crisis has also encouraged local companies to exploit this sentiment in order to launch attacks on multinational competitors.

There are three strategies that can be applied by a company to meet the changes in consumer trends and behavior.[17] These strategies are generic in nature, in that they can be applied equally effectively to any kind of manufacturing industry, producing either consumer or industrial goods, or to any service industry. The first strategy is *maintaining the brand*, which involves upholding the image and reputation of a product in an effort to maintain its "perceived quality" as the basis for strong customer loyalty. The second strategy is *downscaling*, targeting a lower market segment while ensuring that brand equity is not undermined. The third strategy is called *fighter branding*. This strategy is similar to the second strategy in that it involves targeting lower segments. In this case, however, a new brand is created so that the equity of existing brands is not adversely affected.

These three strategies are created to anticipate the *market downscaling* phenomenon, whereby the quality-oriented customers tend to "drop a level" to become value-oriented customers, while the previously value-oriented customers become price-oriented customers.

Strategy 1: Maintaining the Brand

Maintaining the brand is a strategy most suitable for products that already enjoy relatively high brand equity. Such products are usually found at premium markets and appeal to the quality-oriented segment. There will be big risks if they are remodeled to target a lower economic group. Their quality will decline, and consumer perception of their reputation and quality may easily suffer. In times of crisis, it is far safer if such products heighten their efforts to maintain current perceptions of quality and concentrate on targeting only quality-oriented consumers. The hardest task here is thus choosing a marketing strategy aimed at preserving brand equity — especially its "perceived" quality — so that the product is in no way compromised.

Choosing this strategy may present companies with a dilemma, since in a crisis there is a general tendency for "upscale" consumers to lose their quality-oriented focus owing to their decreased buying power. Nevertheless, this does not mean that quality-oriented consumers disappear completely. There will still be a market for such consumers, albeit a smaller one than previously however bad the economic situation becomes. Consumers who are used to buying high-quality products in earlier "boom" times will stick to old habits, and actively resist switching to products of inferior quality.

A suitable positioning strategy for this consumer segment is what we call *romancing the brand*. With this strategy, a company must convince the consumer that its offerings will not lose even the tiniest fraction of their quality and image in times of crisis. The perceived quality of a product should be constantly preserved or even improved upon. This can be achieved by improving the context of a product. In a fine hotel, for instance, free breakfast or late check-out can be offered. The perceived quality of the product in the eyes of consumers must be steadfastly upheld.

The product should be targeted at the upscale, quality-oriented segment of the market. Although this segment becomes smaller during the crisis, adopting this strategy will produce very loyal customers provided that it is implemented well.

The company might even consider raising its prices. The price increase would serve to highlight this differentiation. Efforts to maintain and strengthen differentiation, however, might focus more on the product itself, service, people, or image. Only if the product's content and context are improved upon will consumers continue to respect the product and thereby ensure that its perceived quality remains high.

In designing the appropriate marketing mix, a company must ensure that the high price reflects its good value. It may, for example, offer an "extra package" with the product. As far as promotion is concerned, customer loyalty programs will form the backbone of the company's bid to ensure that its customers do not run to competitors targeting lower segments of the market. Excelcomindo, an Indonesian cellular telephone operator, for example, formed GSM-XL Club to retain its best customers. As for place, a company needs to optimize its existing distribution and marketing channels.

Because this strategy targets the premium segment, a company has no choice but to improve its service to customers. The company has three choices of how to do this. First, it can improve service and raise price simultaneously (*more for more*). Secondly, it can improve service while maintaining price (*more for the same*) (see Box 6.2). And thirdly, it can improve service and reduce price simultaneously (*more for less*). The last choice is the most effective with customers but the most costly to implement.

For process, the company must focus on improving its quality. Efforts at re-engineering, internal or external mergers, product innovation, and strategic alliances (even with competitors) need to be considered in order to maintain or even improve quality. With all these strategies, the company will be able to safeguard the perceived quality and image of its brand(s).

Box 6.2

Singapore Airlines Solidifies its Brand

Already the strongest regional airline before the Asian crisis, Singapore Airlines (SIA) has emerged from the recession even stronger by turning the crisis into opportunity. It strengthened its brand by continually improving its excellence in service and process. While other Asian carriers (many of them debt-laden or money-losing) reduced their services, SIA increased its flights to America, Europe, India, and Australia. It also spent US$292 million upgrading its service in all classes, from offering sleeper seats and gourmet meals in first class, to providing seat-back TV screens and free champagne in economy class — without raising fares.

This strategy is paying off: the airline's load factor (passenger and cargo carried relative to capacity) increased to 75% in the first quarter of 1999 from 70% in the same period in 1998. It is the highest load factor in Asia and among the world's top ten. The increase is not just a reflection of the incipient regional recovery, but an indication that SIA is winning market share over other airlines. SIA also solidified its brand with the strategy. It topped a list of ten most recognized Asian brands (excluding Japan) ranked by Interbrand, an international branding consultancy.

Source: S. Jayasankaran, "Gaining speed," *Far Eastern Economic Review*, July 1, 1999.

Strategy 2: Downscaling

A *downscaling* strategy is aimed at serving the value-oriented consumers. Owing to reduced buying power, many Asian consumers from the quality-oriented segment "fell" to the already big value-oriented segment. Meanwhile, few value-oriented consumers became price-oriented. The value-oriented consumers tend to stick to discount retail outlets, which offer a large variety of products at competitive prices. The value-oriented consumers are not motivated by only low prices; they are interested in both low prices and high quality. The value-oriented segment, due to its size and growth, represents the best prospect during times of crisis; it can also be the hardest to satisfy, since it is composed of mainly "smart" customers.

Effective positioning in the downscaling strategy is to explain to customers that the reduction in product quality is a rational move to make the price more affordable. The company should explain that the price-quality balance is maintained. Rationalizing to the customers carries with it a considerable risk for the company's or product's image and reputation. The customer may become confused by the new positioning. There may also be a cannibal effect if the downscaling is affected by the launch of "sub-brands." Even worse, the product may be irreversibly perceived as low-class. The last situation will leave the company with a difficult situation, especially if it intends to use the downscaling strategy only during the crisis. Thus, determining the appropriate positioning when employing this strategy is critical; a company must ensure that its product's image and reputation remain intact.

In downscaling, the "content" of a company's product may be maintained or reduced (for example, by introducing "mini" or single-use packages). When reducing the product's "content," however, the company needs to maintain the product's quality. Lux — a soap product of Unilever — provides a good illustration. Unilever recently introduced a 60-gram soap bar to replace its old 100-gram bar, naturally at a reduced price, so that its customers could still afford to buy and use the "soap of the stars" (Lux's positioning in several Asian markets).

Another differentiation tactic is to maintain the product's "content" while reducing the "context." This tactic is effective since, as a result of the crisis, more and more consumers are rejecting good packaging ideas or prestigious outlets in favor of product content. An example of context reduction can be seen in the case of mineral water. The cost of packaging mineral water (which is higher than the cost of processing the water itself) can be reduced by using lower-quality bottles or by providing refills for large bottles, without lessening the quality of the water itself.

What about the marketing mix? The company's product must adopt a "bundling" technique. For instance, a company can introduce "three for the price of two" types of offers. Bundling contains smaller risks than offering discounts, because discounts generally tend to have an adverse effect on a product's image (and also on brand equity). Unilever in Thailand put this technique to good use with their Lux soap product, offering a free bar of soap with every six purchased. Since the value-oriented segment has become more sensitive to price concerns, pricing policy and strategy needs to be implemented with care. The price should reflect, as far as possible, the quality offered by the product. The price should give the consumer the best possible value. With regard to promotion, "below-the-line activity" will be the most suitable technique. Meanwhile, "place" must involve a widening of the marketing channel. Selling products through discount stores or "category-killers" must be considered seriously, since value-oriented consumers tend to buy products from outlets offering the lowest price.

The hardest job in implementing the downscaling strategy is to maintain the perceived quality of a product despite the fact that it is now being sold to lower segments. It must be remembered that price tends to act as a "positioning cue"[18] — the cheaper the product, the more likely it is to be viewed as a lower-class product. Thus, the challenge is to avoid this perception in the mind of the consumer. With regard to service, we have two options: same-for-less service, or less-for-less service. These two service strategies need not affect brand equity. Finally, regarding process, the company should consider re-engineering as a way to improve product delivery.

Strategy 3: Fighter Branding

Fighter branding strategy is aimed at penetrating the price-oriented segment, which has become more attractive as a result of the crisis. *Fighter branding* strategy is implemented by creating an entirely new product or range of products under a new brand name (fighter brands). It avoids diluting the perceived quality of the company's existing brands, since there is no connection between the image of the original products (the "parent brand") and that of the new brands. However, this strategy has the major drawback of requiring large resources to create a completely new brand.

Under this strategy, the positioning should aim to plant the message in the minds of consumers that the brand offers good quality at a very affordable price. The brand is not only cheap, but also offers good value to consumers.

As for differentiation, since the focus here is low price, the content and context of a company's product must be reduced. This results in low levels of both actual quality and perceived quality (that is, in the minds of consumers). However, since a new brand is created, the reductions would have no effect on the perceived quality of the original brand. With regard to selling, "feature-selling," involving product offers, is a sufficient persuasion for the price-oriented consumers, who are generally less demanding. The most important element of the marketing mix will be pricing. Pricing strategy should aim at ensuring and maintaining the lowest possible price for the product. On the promotion side, the company should exploit the power of word-of-mouth as a way of cutting promotion costs.

As for process, the company needs to focus on simplifying the distribution chain and cutting logistical costs by adopting a "just-in-time" policy. Finally, for the service aspect, any reduction in customer service will naturally help to keep costs to a minimum.

This strategy was implemented by Wings, one of the largest Indonesian consumer product companies. Seeing the declining purchasing power of Indonesian consumers, Wings launched a "crisis" brand, Daia, to complement its leading detergent, So-Klin. By using lower-quality ingredients, Wings was able to price Daia well below other major detergent brands like Unilever's Rinso and Kao's Attack. Daia immediately reaped success, since it offered great value to Indonesia's large price-oriented segment during the crisis.

The Strategic Scorecard

All concepts in the strategic business architecture are basically aimed at creating value for the three main stakeholders of a company: customers, employees, and shareholders.[19] As shown in Figure 6.6, value offers happen in several ways. The company offers "value-packages" in order to acquire the right buyers, recruit the right workers, and attract the right investors. In reverse, buyers, workers, and investors also offer value to the company as they buy, work, and invest. Therefore, a company actually competes in the 3C markets: the competency market, the commercial market, and the capital market (see Figure 6.7). Given this, the strategic business architecture should be "marketed" to the commercial market by offering value to buyers, to the competency market for workers, and to the capital market for investors.

Once the "transactions" occur, buyers become customers, workers become employees, and investors become shareholders. The company then tries to convert them into loyal customers, committed people, and long-term shareholders. If the company succeeds, they will "guard" the company against the other potential stakeholders, such as government, the media, competitors, financial institutions, non-government organizations (NGOs), labor unions, creditors, and the community.

There are three stages of what a company should do to serve its customers. "Customers" here also includes employees, who are internal customers, and shareholders, who are investor customers. First, the company must offer one particular value to acquire these customers. Second, it must create customer

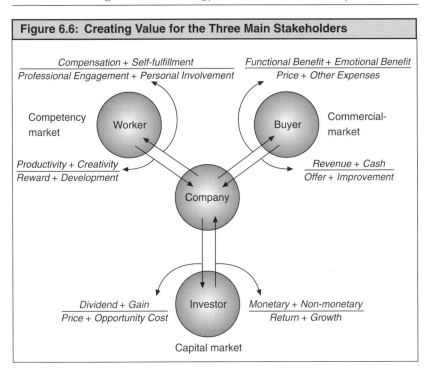

Figure 6.6: Creating Value for the Three Main Stakeholders

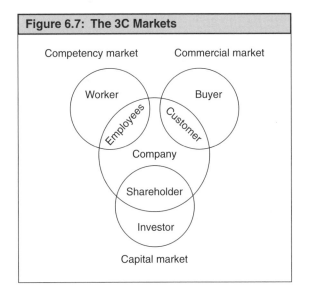

Figure 6.7: The 3C Markets

satisfaction by delivering value as promised. And third, it must retain its customers by enhancing value from time to time.

There should also be a balance among the customer value, employee value, and shareholder value. Each component should be measured and monitored.[20] The performance indicator includes two dimensions: *value levers* and *value risks*. A company must control the value lever and monitor the value risk of each customer (see Figure 6.8). The value lever is a performance indicator that is controllable by the company, such as customer satisfaction, return on investment, and employee satisfaction index. Value risk, on the other hand, refers to things that a company cannot control, such as customer turnover, market sentiment indicator, and employee turnover. Since value risk indicators are uncontrollable, the company should monitor them closely.

The Enterprise Sub-model

A company may have an activity system and analytical tools like the 3Cs and TOWS, but it will still need three other inputs: inspiration, (the right) corporate culture, and institution.

Inspiration

A company is set up not only to achieve profits, but also to enact a certain ideology or philosophy. As shown in Figure 6.9, the company's mission and vision are put on the philosophy side, while business (scope) and goals are put on the objective side. A mission statement defines "what business you are in" and is translated into a more concrete business scope. Vision defines "the desired future destination" and leads to the business goal. The hour-glass illustration reflects that the time will come for a "reckoning" and that a company's inspiration must be redefined and adjusted to the business environment from time to time.

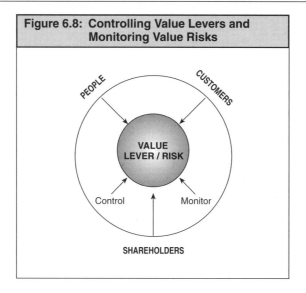

Figure 6.8: Controlling Value Levers and Monitoring Value Risks

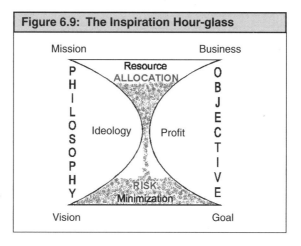

Figure 6.9: The Inspiration Hour-glass

The South Korean *chaebols* are a good example of companies that need to redefine their inspiration. In the pre-crisis era, the *chaebols* tried to offer "everything to everybody." Since facing financial difficulties as a result of the crisis, the *chaebols* are being pressured to restructure and refocus their businesses. In these efforts, they must re-evaluate their mission and vision, as well as their business scope and goals.

Corporate Culture

A new business strategy usually entails a new organization design. Once the new organization design has been formulated, a new, strong corporate culture needs to be built. Corporate culture plays the important roles of directing employees' behavior in the organization in the right direction. Corporate culture is also the binding force in an organization.

As argued by John Kotter, there are two components of corporate culture: shared values (cognitive), and common behavior (psychomotor).[21] Shared values are the denominating values held by people in the organization and are usually static, since they usually remain the same over time (unless a radical change occurs). Common behavior, on the other hand, changes from time to time in line with changes in the organization and environment.

Collins and Porras, in *Built to Last*, argue that shared values and common behavior should go hand in hand.[22] A company equipped with a beautifully written shared values statement is nothing without a consistent common behavior of the employees. In reverse, even though it is better to have appropriate behavior, it will be dangerous for the company's continuity if there is no "basic inspiration" for the behavior. Thus, just like the yin-yang philosophy, the two must be in "harmony" if a company wants to build a solid corporate culture (see Figure 6.10).

Institution

Efforts to survive will depend on management and measurement[23] (see Figure 6.11). Organization is the "vehicle" to carry out the mission. The organization must have a clear target and set measurable milestones to check the balance for the main stakeholders (customers, employees, and shareholders). The crucial thing in an organization is work coordination. Therefore, the structure and system should be properly set to facilitate work coordination in order to maximize the return.

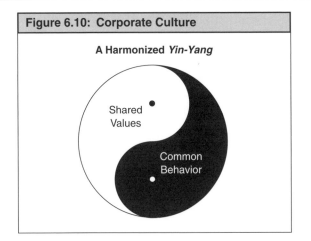

Figure 6.10: Corporate Culture

A Harmonized *Yin-Yang*

Shared Values

Common Behavior

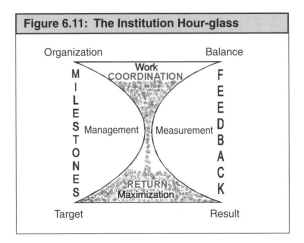

Figure 6.11: The Institution Hour-glass

Organization | Balance

MILESTONES

Work COORDINATION

Management | Measurement

RETURN Maximization

FEEDBACK

Target | Result

Putting It All Together

In Figure 6.12, the three sub-models are combined into one comprehensive model. If a company drives itself through the infinity-sustainability loop, it must re-do the outlook, architecture, and scorecard. At the same time, it must review the inspiration, culture, and institution, and adapt them if warranted.

The Asian crisis has affected every company in the region. Most Asian companies have no choice but to restructure and rethink their strategies. Such companies can use the sustainable

Figure 6.12: The Comprehensive Sustainable Marketing Enterprise Model

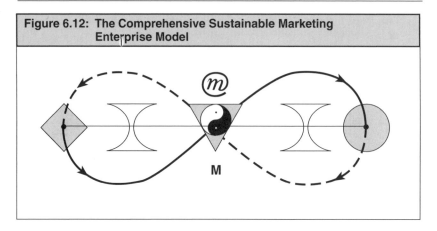

marketing enterprise model not only to survive the crisis, but also to achieve a more sustainable prosperity. By using the model, Asian companies will be reminded of the factors needed to formulate an effective business strategy and build strong management systems through both good times and bad.

1   Value migrators are change drivers that cause value shifts within industry. See Adrian J. Slywotzky, *Value Migration: How to Think Several Moves Ahead of the Competition* (Boston: HBS Press, 1996).

2   McKinsey & Co., "Responding to the Economic Crisis in South-East Asia: Risks and Opportunities for Multinational Corporations," April 1998.

3   Ibid.

4   Ibid.

5   Philip Kotler, *Marketing Management*, 4th edition (Englewood Cliffs, N.J.: Prentice Hall, 1980), p. 434.

6   See Hermawan Kartajaya, I. Putu Mandau Wijayanto, and Yuswohady, "Consumer behavior in the economic crisis and its implication for marketing strategy," *Kelola: Gajah Mada University Business Review*, No. 18/VII/1998, pp. 104–136.

7   See Taufik, "On becoming the most admired regional cement player," *MarkPlus Quarterly*, Vol. 2, No. 2 (1999), pp. 48–55.

8   Quoted from Michael Porter, "What is strategy?" *Harvard Business Review*, November–December 1996.

9   Quoted from Michael Alan Hamlin, *Asia's Best: The Myth and Reality of Asia's Most Successful Companies* (Singapore: Prentice Hall, 1998), p. 135.

10   Philip Kotler, *Kotler on Marketing: How to Create, Win, and Dominate Markets* (New York: The Free Press, 1999), pp. 59–61.

11   Fara Warner, "Building a brand," *The Asian Wall Street Journal's Asian Economic Survey 1996–1997*, pp. 26–27.

12   Leslie Chang, "Making a name," *The Asian Wall Street Journal's Asian Economic Survey 1996–1997*, p. 27.

13   Quoted from Philip Kotler, *Marketing Management*, 9th edition (Englewood Cliffs, N.J.: Prentice Hall, 1997), p. 443.

14   Warner, "Building a brand," op. cit.

15   Contributed by Professor Rajendra Srivastava, University of Texas, Austin.

16   See "Asia's sinking middle class," *Far Eastern Economic Review*, April 8, 1998.

17   This section draws heavily on Hermawan Kartajaya et al., "Consumer behavior in the economic crisis ...," op. cit.

18   A full description of the negative effects of a downscaling strategy on brand equity can be found in David Aaker, *Building Strong Brand* (New York: The Free Press, 1996).

19   Other important stakeholders may include supplier partners and distribution partners.

20   Robert Kaplan and David Norton, *Balanced Scorecard* (Boston: HBS Press, 1996).

21   John Kotter, *Leading Change* (Boston: HBS Press, 1996).

22   James Collins and Jerry Porras, *Built to Last* (New York: HarperCollins, 1994).

23   Kaplan and Norton, *Balanced Scorecard*, op. cit.

CHAPTER 7

THE 3CS FORMULA FOR MNCS

For many years, Asia's strong record of growth and macroeconomic stability have made it an attractive investment destination for multinational companies. When the United States and Europe faced slow growth and rising unemployment, the lure of outsized earnings growth in Asia was simply irresistible to these MNCs, especially when combined with low taxes, no (visible) fiscal problems, a flexible labor force, stable currencies, and pro-business governments.[1]

When the crisis hit Asia, the region's currencies and stock markets fell sharply, changing the once stable environment into an uncertain one. With the devaluing Asian currencies (and thus, the strengthening US dollar), several MNCs lost competitiveness in the Asian markets as their products or services often became unaffordable by Asian consumers whose purchasing power had declined sharply. In a survey conducted by Andersen Consulting in April 1998, most multinational respondents anticipated a big fall in sales (61% of respondents) and profits (57% of respondents).[2] Most of the MNCs surveyed, however, were in a much better position compared to their domestic counterparts. Only 18% of the multinational respondents faced liquidity problems and 4% faced heavy debt burdens. Meanwhile, the proportions of Asian companies' respondents that faced liquidity problems and heavy debt burdens were 50% and 32%, respectively. Yet, despite the depth of the crisis, many MNCs still perceive opportunity in the region.[3]

In fact, the crisis actually represents a discontinuity that is opening up acquisition and business building opportunities that did not exist previously. The longer-term impact of Asian countries' reform programs is likely to be favorable to MNCs as there will be less government interference, greater transparency, and stronger legal and financial systems (provided that reform programs are implemented as planned). Changes in regulation, competition, and consumer preferences can also offer greater opportunities to capture synergy and reshape industry. For example, opportunities to capture sales synergies will be easier to obtain, as domestic partners may be more open to co-branding or broadening product lines due to their poor bargaining position. Opportunity also exists for consolidating industry and taking a leadership position. This is especially true when foreign ownership limitations are reduced in many Asian countries while domestic companies are in greater need of capital. These changes presented many MNCs with opportunities to acquire or take a controlling stake in Asian companies facing financial distress.

As an example, Coca-Cola is positioning itself to increase its market share by acquiring its bottlers in South Korea, where it invested US$500 million to acquire 100% of its South Korean bottler, and Thailand, where it invested US$50 million to acquire 49% of its Thai bottler.[4] Multinational banks are already on a buying spree in Indonesia.[5] Foreign banks, which are relatively well off, are taking advantage of the opportunities to buy out vulnerable Indonesian local banks (especially those under the state-led recapitalization program), which have been experiencing negative spreads since the beginning of the crisis. Foreign ownership in Indonesia's banking industry is expected to be between 20% and 25% in the country's post-election period, compared to only 7% prior to the election. And, as illustrated in Box 7.1, GE Capital is accelerating its acquisitions of Asian finance companies during the crisis.

Box 7.1

GE Capital: King of the Crisis

Although GE Capital has had a presence in several Asian countries since the mid-1990s, mostly in the form of joint ventures (JVs), it didn't start making major investments in the region until the crisis hit. Falling asset prices and Asian companies' desperation for cash had been the main factors.

Starting in 1997, GE began their search to find acquisition targets, often pursuing less-glamorous, but potentially profitable, financial-services businesses such as leasing, life insurance, and consumer credit. Since 1998, GE Capital has spent an astonishing US$15 billion on distressed assets in recession-plagued Asia (see Box Figure 7.1). When it acquired Japan Leasing Corp. (worth US$7 billion), almost overnight GE Capital became a major financial-services player in Japan. It has also snapped up cheap assets from Thailand to the Philippines. GE expects that Asia-based businesses will generate 10% of its global earnings by 2001, up from an estimated 1% in 1997.

The company's plunge into Asia resembled its strategy in Europe in the mid-1990s. Taking advantage of recession and industry restructuring, GE Capital snapped up a host of European targets; to date, it has invested more than US$23 billion in European operations.

GE Capital began in 1932 by providing consumer loans for the products made by its parent, General Electric. Since then, it has mushroomed into a financial conglomerate embracing 28 distinct businesses ranging from car and aircraft financing to real estate and mortgage services. More than 300 acquisitions made worldwide since 1988 have turned GE Capital into the world's largest non-bank financial company, with assets of over US$300 billion, or 40% of General Electric's net

---

Box Figure 7.1: GE Capital's Spending in Asia

Country	Price tag (US$ million)	Recent investments	Areas GE Capital is eyeing for future investment
Japan	7,000	Japan Leasing Corp.	Commercial finance
	4,300	Lake Co.	Specialty leasing
	900	Toho/GE Edison Life	Consumer finance
	N.A.	Koel Credit (Dec. 1997)	
Thailand	1,100	Restructuring-agency Loans (with Goldman Sachs)	Banking Consumer finance
	N.A.	Central Card Co.	
	10	Asia Finance Public Co.	
	N.A.	GS Capital Corp.	
Indonesia	N.A.	GE Astra Finance	Banking consumer finance
South Korea	N.A.	Korea First Bank—pending (with Newbridge Capital)	Loan portfolios
Philippines	N.A.	Philippine Asia Life	
Hong Kong	N.A.	Various loan portfollos	Banking vehicle leasing Consumer finance

Sources: Far Eastern Economic Review; GE Capital.

earnings. GE Capital has produced a return on equity of around 20% in each of the last 20 years.

Source: "GE Capital: King of crisis," Far Eastern Economic Review, May 6, 1999.

Multinational companies have the advantage over Asian companies in dominating various markets or industries in Asia. The Asian crisis has essentially destroyed the high entry barriers in many Asian countries, many of which need help and investments from the West to rekindle their economies.

With all these advantages and opportunities, however, MNCs must also gradually become true members of "Corporate Asia." They must become more "responsible" to the region by participating in realizing Asia's vision of becoming a sustainable economic region. MNCs that are concerned about their long-term prospects must adapt themselves to Asian conditions and contribute to the overall development of Asia.

"The End of Corporate Imperialism"[6]

C.K. Prahalad and Kenneth Lieberthal pointed out that multinationals must adopt a new way of thinking if they want to succeed in emerging markets. In the past, despite the uncertainty and difficulty of doing business in emerging markets such as Asia and Latin America, Western MNCs had no choice but to enter these markets. The lure of a vast consumer base of hundreds of millions of people that is developing rapidly is simply too hard to ignore as the MNCs searched for growth opportunities. During the first wave of market entry in the 1980s, many MNCs operated with an "imperialist mind-set." They assumed that the big emerging markets were new markets for their old products. Entering the emerging markets was seen as a chance to squeeze profits out of their sunset technologies. Furthermore, the corporate headquarters was seen as the center of product and process innovation. Few, if any, MNCs seriously considered the emerging markets as sources of technical and managerial talent for their global operations. The authors argued that as a result of this imperialist mind-set, multinationals have achieved only limited success in the emerging markets.

Nowadays, MNCs have to realize that succeeding in the big emerging markets will require more than developing cultural sensitivity. Instead, due to the diverse and unique nature of these markets, MNCs will have to review and reconfigure every element of their business models. In fact, "success in the emerging markets will require innovation and resource shifts on such a scale that life within the multinationals themselves will inevitably be transformed." In short, to achieve success in the emerging markets, MNCs have to bring an end to their imperialist mind-sets.

Prahalad and Lieberthal believe that there are five basic issues that MNCs must address if they are to compete successfully in the big emerging markets:

- Who is the emerging middle-class market in these countries, and what kind of business model will effectively serve their needs?
- What are the key characteristics of the distribution networks in these markets, and how are the networks evolving?
- What mix of local and global leadership is required to foster business opportunities?
- Should the MNC adopt a consistent strategy for all its business units within one country?
- Will local partners accelerate the multinational's ability to learn about the market?

What is the Business Model for the Emerging Middle Class?

Although it is true that middle-class consumers in the emerging markets "have entered a new era of product and availability and choice," MNCs must look closer into the market structure. When Western managers hear about the emerging markets' middle class, they often think in terms of the middle class in developed countries like Europe and the United States. The fact is, while it is true that consumers in the emerging markets today are more affluent than in the past, they are not affluent by Western standards. Income levels that characterize the Western middle class would represent a tiny upper class of consumers in the emerging markets. Today, active consumers in emerging markets have a three-tiered pyramid structure, as shown in Figure 7.1.

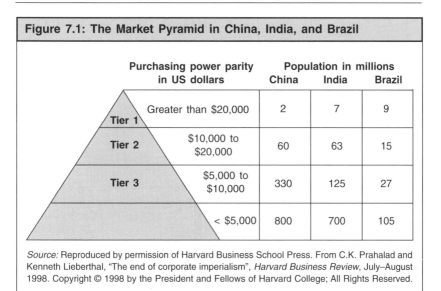

Figure 7.1: The Market Pyramid in China, India, and Brazil

	Purchasing power parity in US dollars	Population in millions China	India	Brazil
Tier 1	Greater than $20,000	2	7	9
Tier 2	$10,000 to $20,000	60	63	15
Tier 3	$5,000 to $10,000	330	125	27
	< $5,000	800	700	105

Source: Reproduced by permission of Harvard Business School Press. From C.K. Prahalad and Kenneth Lieberthal, "The end of corporate imperialism", *Harvard Business Review*, July–August 1998. Copyright © 1998 by the President and Fellows of Harvard College; All Rights Reserved.

At the top of the pyramid, in Tier 1, is a relatively small number of consumers who are responsive to international brands and have the income to afford them. In Tier 2, there is a larger group of consumers who are less attracted to international brands. Finally, at the bottom of the pyramid, in Tier 3, there is a huge group of people who are loyal to local customs and habits, and, often, local brands. Below these three tiers is another huge group of people who are unlikely to become active consumers anytime soon.

As a result of a lack of understanding of this market structure, MNCs often fail to adapt their products and marketing strategies to the local situation. Consequently, they end up becoming high-end niche players serving only Tier 1 of the pyramid.[7] To address this issue, MNCs must do more than make minor cultural adaptations or marginal cost reductions. Instead, they must rethink every element of their business model, which includes the price-performance equation, brand management, costs of market building, product design, packaging, and capital efficiency.

How does the Distribution System Work?

A good understanding of the emerging markets' distribution systems is a crucial factor for the success of MNCs. Distribution in China, for example, is primarily local and provincial. In this former planned economy, most distribution networks were confined to political units, such as counties, cities, or provinces. Even today, there is no real national distribution network for most products. In India, on the other hand, individual entrepreneurs have already put together a national distribution system in a wide variety of businesses. The system takes the form of long-standing arrangements with networks of small-scale distributors throughout the country, and the banking network is part of those relationships. The differences between the distribution systems in India and China alone should send signals to MNCs that they must adapt their approaches to local conditions.

Will Local or Expatriate Leadership be More Effective?

Leadership of a multinational's venture in an emerging market requires a complex blend of local sensitivity and global knowledge. Striking a balance between the two is both crucial and perplexing. MNCs frequently lack the cultural understanding to get the right mix of expatriate and local leaders. While expatriates from the MNC's host country play significant roles such as transfer of technology, management practices, and corporate culture, local managers are also instrumental in having a good appreciation of local nuances. This issue must be resolved depending on the MNC's particular needs within each country.[8]

Is it Necessary to "Present One Face"?

Due to local political considerations, MNCs often have to decide whether to adopt a uniform strategy for each of its business units operating in the country or to permit each unit to act on its own. In China, massive governmental interference in the economy makes a uniform country strategy necessary, since the Chinese government tends to view the activities of individual business units as part of a single company's effort. Therefore, concessions made by any one unit — such as an agreement to achieve a certain level of local sourcing — may well become requirements for the others. A multinational in China must be able to articulate a set of principles that conforms to China's announced priorities, and it should coordinate the activities of its various business units so that they resonate with those priorities. In India, on the other hand, there is somewhat less need to "present one face". The Indian government has scaled back its efforts to shape what MNCs do in the country. Business units may therefore act more independently than would be appropriate in China.

Do Partners Foster Valuable Learning?

In the first stage of market entry, multinationals often formed joint ventures (JV) with local partners, which helped them to learn about the new markets. However, tensions often occur in JV relationships. The JV relationship, as one Chinese manager said, is often like "sleeping in the same bed, but having different dreams." When MNCs come to an emerging market, they usually are still building their manufacturing and marketing infrastructures, and they do not expect immediate returns. Local partners, on the other hand, often want to see short-term profit and transfer of technology.

"Who controls what" can be yet another source of trouble — especially when the domestic partner has experience in the business. And when new investment is needed to grow the business, local partners often are unable to bring in the matching funds, yet they resent the dilution of their holding and the ensuing loss of control.

In recent years, however, the MNCs' need for local partners is clearly diminishing, especially in Asia where markets are becoming more open to foreigners. In 1997, a consulting firm surveyed 67 companies investing in China and found that the percentage of their projects that became wholly foreign-owned enterprises grew steadily from 18% in 1992 to 37% in 1996.

The 3Cs Formula: A Strategic Business Triangle System for MNCs

If one considers the issues raised by Prahalad and Lieberthal, achieving success in Asia will not be easy, due to the many complexities that are present in the region. Multinationals will have to reconfigure their resource base, rethink their cost structure, and redesign their process to fit the unique Asian business environment. Most importantly, MNCs need to review and renew their business models.

Multinational companies must strike a careful balance between standardization and local effectiveness. Standardization would promote more efficiency and consistency in managing global operations. Professor Theodore Levitt of Harvard University has supplied the intellectual rationale for global standardization.[9] He wrote:

> The world is becoming a common marketplace in which people — no matter where they live — desire the same products and lifestyles. Global companies must forget the idiosyncratic differences between countries and cultures and instead concentrate on satisfying universal drives.[10]

Levitt believes that new communication and transportation technologies have created a more homogeneous world market. People around the world want the same basic things — products that make life easier and increase their discretionary time and buying power. In effect, this convergence of needs and wants has created global markets for standardized products. Thus, global marketers must realize that substantial economies will be achieved through standardization of production,

212

distribution, marketing, and management. The economies of scale will be translated into greater value for consumers by offering high quality and more reliable products at a lower price.

Others feel that consumer needs vary and that marketing programs will be more effective when tailored to each customer target group in different countries. Current developments and conditions in various emerging markets have called for more adaptation. Adaptation may be done on product features, labeling, packaging, colors, materials, prices, advertising, and sales promotion.[11]

When considering adaptation versus standardization, a company needs to think in terms of incremental revenue versus incremental cost.[12] That is, rather than assuming that the company's domestic product can be introduced as is in another country, the company should review all possible adaptation elements and determine which adaptations would add more revenue than cost. By thinking this way, a balance can be struck between the two extremes, as companies can decide which elements to standardize and which elements to adapt to local markets.

One way of creating an effective business model is to create an appropriate strategic business triangle system. To review this subject, a strategic business triangle system consists of corporate strategies, corporate tactics, and corporate values that will serve as a platform for a company's activities. We propose that multinationals operating in Asia, or in any other emerging markets, adopt consistent global value, coordinated regional strategy, and customized local tactics (see Figure 7.2). By doing this, a company can standardize certain core elements and localize other elements. Let's look at each element in turn.

Consistent Global Value

As explained in the previous chapter, corporate value consists of the three elements of brand, service, and process. Among the three components of the strategic business triangle system,

Figure 7.2: The 3Cs Formula for MNCs

	Strategy	Tactic	Value
Global (World)			Consistent Global Value
Regional (Asia)	Coordinated Regional Strategy		
Local (Country)		Customized Local Tactic	

corporate value is the one component that should be standardized. This is due to the high cost of investments and time in developing excellence in each element of the corporate value. Furthermore, a worldwide recognized brand name is a power in itself, especially when the country-of-origin associations are highly respected. For instance, Procter & Gamble and Unilever have developed a global reputation for quality and a wide assortment of consumer products. Their names on products give buyers instant confidence that they are getting good value.

True, some global brands require some adjustment to local conditions. However, most of the adaptations that should be done are in the form of the brand's communications, labeling, packaging, and advertising, all of which fall under the configuration of corporate tactics (especially marketing mix).

Maintaining and building global brand equity takes a great deal of time and investment. For example, Miller Brewery spent US$50 million to launch a new brand of beer called "Miller Regular" in the United States. Then, once the brand is "born" (in the minds of consumers), it needs consistent advertising to build brand acceptability, brand preference, and brand loyalty. In his book *22 Immutable Laws of Branding*, Al Ries comments:

"[Brand] advertising budget is like a country's defense budget." That is, the massive spending on brand advertising does not buy a company anything; it just keeps the company or product from losing market share to its competition.

Brand-building requires more than just designing a logo and spending massive amounts on advertising. To build and maintain strong brand equity, a company also needs to excel in service (the value enhancer) and process (the value enabler).

Developing global service consistency and process excellence requires a great amount of effort and investment. With lots of investment, McDonald's has been very successful in providing consistent service around the world. Clean restaurants, convenience, and employees' courtesy can be found in any McDonald's outlet. To achieve this, McDonald's designs high standards and procedures/processes to be followed by its franchisees around the world. It even trains its franchisees at McDonald's own Hamburger University. As a result, McDonald's customers in Mumbai (formerly Bombay), Beijing, and Jakarta receive the same service.

Information technology (which is part of developing efficient process) is another area needing standardization due to its high cost. Most MNCs have set up worldwide intranet systems to facilitate information flows among their employees/divisions around the world.

Coordinated Regional Strategy

As explained in Chapter 3, the Asian crisis is transforming Asia from the "flying geese" structure into a more regionalized structure, in which several "economic regions" will be formed (ASEAN, Greater China, SAARC, and so on). With this new structure, MNCs certainly cannot view Asia as a single, uniform market. There is a great deal of diversity among the countries within each economic region. Within ASEAN, for example, the Jakarta and Singapore markets are very different demographically, even though the two cities are only 90 minutes by air from each other. Whereas Singapore is dominated by ethnic Chinese, Indonesians are predominantly Muslims. However, tailoring strategies and operations for each Asian country to the full extent would require too great an investment in supply chains and offices.

To accommodate both strategy effectiveness and efficiency, multinationals can coordinate their strategies and operations at the regional level. Segmentation, targeting, and positioning can be conducted either at the global or regional level. However, there should also be a regional strategy that will ensure both the consistency of the company's global value and its adaptation to each local market. McDonald's is a good example of an MNC that coordinates its strategy at the regional level. McDonald's is famous for its Big Mac. However, after studying Asians' fast-food preferences, it decided to offer fried chicken in several Asian countries. The fried-chicken product is then tailored to local tastes while maintaining its standards. For instance, in Indonesia, where people like spicy foods, it introduced McChicken, which is served with more spice.

On the operations side, MNCs can optimize their effectiveness and efficiency by translating and reconfiguring their global operating model at the regional level. They can set up a regional head office in each economic region that will coordinate the activities of representative offices in each country. In ASEAN, for example, the regional office can be located in Singapore, which many people consider the financial and trading hub of Southeast Asia. For Greater China, Hong Kong can be chosen as the regional headquarters, while in SAARC, Mumbai or New Delhi can serve as the regional hub. Then, factories can be set up to serve each economic region or the whole Asian region, depending on the market demand and the appropriate efficiency level. Optimization can also be done for warehouses, marketing and sales offices, and billing offices. By reconfiguring their operating models, MNCs can still maintain efficiency while taking into account Asia's diversity. Several successful MNCs in Asia have done this. Ericsson, for example, came up with a new global operating model that will increase efficiency in order delivery and payment flows. To ensure its effectiveness, the company adjusts the model to each region's specific conditions and regulations. In China, for instance, it routes its invoice flows according to Chinese regulations that prohibit the attachment of invoices to shipments of products.

Customized Local Tactics

Corporate tactics, which consist of differentiation, marketing mix, and selling, are an element where MNCs have much leeway for customization to suit local or country-specific needs. Differentiation in each local market can be done either in content, context, or infrastructure. Coca-Cola uses content and context differentiation in Asia. In differentiating its content, Coca-Cola makes its products less sweet or less carbonated in several countries in Southeast Asia. Meanwhile, their context differentiation comes in the form of labeling and packaging. In China, for example, the name "Coca-Cola" is written in Chinese characters and pronounced as *gege-gele*, which means "happy drink" in Chinese.

Customization can also be done in configuring a company's or a product's marketing mix, which includes product, price, place, and promotion (the 4Ps). McDonald's customizes its products in Asia by tailoring them to local tastes. In Indonesia, they offer several menus that are not available anywhere else, such as McSate (hamburger with a traditional Indonesian BBQ flavor). To cater to victims of the country's economic crisis, it also offers special value-meal packages at a very special price; these are popularly known as *Pa-He*, or "thrift packages." In localizing its place or distribution, McDonald's outlets in several Asian countries usually occupy a very large space and are generally located in crowded areas like shopping malls and popular tourist places. Its main outlet in Beijing, for example, has at least 20 counters serving customers. Finally, in promotion, McDonald's often uses local themes or celebrities in its TV and print-media advertising. In Indonesia, McDonald's features two popular Indonesian MTV-Asia VJs, Jamie Aditya and Sarah Sechan.

Finally, MNCs can customize their selling tactics as needed. Citibank, for example, offers its credit card products in Southeast Asian countries using extensive personal selling. This differs markedly from the company's approach in the United States, where mainly direct mailing is used.

Conclusion

The Asian economic crisis has presented multinational companies with many opportunities to expand their presence in the region. However, as MNCs become more involved in the region, they need to adapt their approach to the region by rethinking and reconfiguring every aspect of their business models. Corporate imperialism is dying.

MNCs that want to truly exploit the huge potential of Asia must increase their "responsibility" by participating in the realization of Asia's vision to become a sustainable economic region. To help realize this vision, MNCs should not just participate in short-term portfolio investments that can be withdrawn from the region whenever there are signs of danger. Instead, MNCs should be involved as "genuine" foreign direct investors, treating Asia not just as a huge market to be exploited, but also as a source of innovation and talent that can return benefits to their home countries.

---

1   McKinsey & Company, "Responding to the Economic Crisis in South-East Asia: Risks and Opportunities for Multinational Corporations," April 1998.
2   Andersen Consulting, "Creating the Breakaway Advantage," April 1998.
3   Ibid.
4   Ibid.
5   "Kredit bermasalah 74 bank Rp. 73 Triliun," *Bisnis Indonesia*, May 11, 1999, p. 1.
6   This section draws heavily on C.K. Prahalad and Kenneth Lieberthal, "The end of corporate imperialism," *Harvard Business Review*, July–August 1998. Reproduced by permission of Harvard Business School Press. Copyright © 1998 by the President and Fellows of Harvard College; All Rights Reserved.
7   For examples, please refer to the article in *Harvard Business Review*.
8   Several sub-issues are discussed in the article.

9   Philip Kotler, "Global Standardization or Adaptation?," *Marketing Management*, 9th edition (Englewood Cliffs, N.J.: Prentice Hall, 1997), pp. 414–15.

10   Quoted from Theodore Levitt, "The globalization of markets," *Harvard Business Review*, May–June 1983, pp. 92–102.

11   Kotler, "Global Standardization or Adaptation?" op. cit.

12   Ibid.

Index